THE NEW BOOK OF SAIL
TRIM

THE NEW BOOK OF SAIL TRIM

Edited by
KEN TEXTOR

ADLARD COLES NAUTICAL
London

Published 1995 by Adlard Coles Nautical,
an imprint of A & C Black (Publishers), Ltd.
35 Bedford Row, London WC1R 4JH

With acknowledgment to the staff of SAIL Magazine

First published in the United States by Sheridan House, Inc. 1995
First published in Great Britain by Adlard Coles Nautical 1995

ISBN 0-7136-4264-5

A CIP catalogue record for this book is available from the British Library.

Production/Design: Lorretta Palagi
Composition: Kathleen Weisel

Printed and bound in the United States of America.

Contents

Introduction

"There's nothing to trimming a sail," a flinty old sailor once told me. "It's just a matter of keeping the sails full of wind. They flap a little and you're doing it wrong. No flapping and you're all set."

As with most simple advice, this is only half right. It's a little like saying falling in love is just ..., well, suffice it to say it just doesn't tell the whole story. But the authors of the articles in this book *do* fill in the rest of the story on trimming, maintaining, and generally getting the most out of sails and sailing. In fact, they discuss aspects of sail trim that have never been explored in a book before.

For instance, in the *Cruising Trim* section there is a wealth of information from which cruising sailors could benefit greatly. Well-known cruisers like Lin and Larry Pardey offer insights into the most maddening aspect of long-distance sailing, light air sailing. After reading it, it's easy to see how they've kept their sanity after thousands of miles chasing zephyrs, ripples and puffs without an engine. Steve Dashew then offers two unique – and in some quarters, controversial – ideas that cruisers could adapt to their own boats. Like the Pardeys, and nearly all cruising sailors I know, Dashew is mostly interested in getting farther faster and easier, controversy notwithstanding. His ideas are therefore well worth considering. Other well-known cruisers join in with equally innovative thoughts and tricks.

Still, it was the *Race Tactics* section of this book that truly opened my eyes. The real pros of sailing never rest with just a good performance. They're always looking for improvement. For instance, Michael Tamulaites of SAIL Magazine has written two masterful descriptions of how to improve your small boat racing. Roll-tacking and roll-gybing are tough to execute well. But with coach

Tamulaites' advice, most readers will be able to approach the problem with new confidence. And big boat racers will also improve their upwind and downwind performances with secrets from old hands Brad Dellenbaugh and Jim Marshall. Interestingly, Dellenbaugh and Marshall both emphasize a discipline of the body *and* the mind to win those close races. Other names you'll probably recognize – Ed Baird, Mike Huck, Derrick Fries, etc. – also offer intriguing tips on top-quality racing in all kinds of wind and sea conditions.

If you're just beginning to sail, however, the basic principles of good performance are crucial. They, too, are carefully examined in the *Some Basics* section. Top racers like Tom Leweck haven't forgotten what it's like to have a jib sheet in your hand for the first time. Step by step, Leweck helps you master that sometimes-mysterious headsail without once letting you know he's raced across the Pacific to Hawaii more times than most of us would care to contemplate. Working aft on the beginner's boat, Mike Toppa explains the nitty-gritty of the genoa, Roger Marshall takes on the intricacies of the mainsail, Jeff Johnstone describes the fundamentals of sail shapes, and four other authors work hard to take the confusion out of the art of sailing. Confidentially, even with 17 years of sailing under my belt, I still picked up a few worthy ideas from this down-to-earth section.

Without question, it was the section titled *Spinnaker Talk* that sometimes had me on the edge of my seat. Much like hurtling along with this formidable sail set, most of the authors have brought some of that breathless adventure of the foredeck to the printed page. Ed Baird leads the pack with his description of how you catch a "tow" from another boat sailing downwind. With your boat perched nearly on the transom of another boat, Baird carefully details the complexities of executing this trick. It's definitely a highwire act. Then Great Lakes sailor Wally Cross discusses asymmetrical spinnakers, which are becoming increasingly popular among cruising sailors as well as long-distance racers. The section winds up with a solid – and sometimes sweet – discussion of basic spinnaker handling by Sally Lindsay, a professional sailmaker and successful West Coast racer.

Of course, no book on sail trim would be complete without a thorough discussion of the revolution that has taken place in sail construction and materials in the last ten years or so. The *New Sail Materials* section does this with six enlightening in-depth discussions, led by SAIL Magazine executive editor Charles Mason. He persuaded six sailmakers to tell him how they would design a fore-sail and mainsail for the average cruising/racing boat. The results were surprisingly varied. Jeff Spranger, too, adds an excellent over-view of what's available in new sail cloths, computerized design-ing and the like. And sailmaker Peter Mahr puts it all under the microscope to let you know the nuts and bolts of what's happen-ing to modern sails.

Finally, most sailors will confess to being at least part-time gear freaks. If you're like me, almost any sail trimming gizmo usu-ally catches my eye. So in the *Gear Tricks* section, I was immedi-ately drawn to Steve Cruse's discussion of the full-batten mainsail and Art Bandy's talk about the uses of a whisker pole. Neither piece of gear is particularly new to a sailor's repertoire. But both authors cast a new light on these old standbys, bringing their value as trimming aids up to date. Even Eric Hall's discussion of the old-time jiffy reefing system made me a little nostalgic for the older – and sometimes more reliable – means of reefing a boat's sails. Sal Fertitta, Bill Gladstone and Larry Montgomery also add some valu-able gear tips.

Ultimately, good sail trimming is a result of constant prac-tice, on your own boat, in as varied conditions as you can find. All the authors in this book repeat this advice over and over. I couldn't agree more. Still it's nice to know such a fine collection of coaches, advisors and mentors can be found – whenever you need them – between the covers of an item as handy as a book.

Ken Textor
Arrowsic Island, Maine
October 1994

I

Some Basics

Handling the Headsail

*Here's some upfront advice about
an adaptable sail*

Tom Leweck

Technological advances in sailing seem to get a lot of emphasis these days. However, it's still the art of sailing – not the science – that provides the satisfaction that attracts so many of us to the water. For most of us, it's hard to beat the pleasure that comes from "doing it right."

Proper headsail handling is an important part of that art, partially because the jib is attached to the boat along only one of its three sides, the luff. The trimmer must adjust all three sides of the sail to set it correctly.

Halyard tension.   Hoist the headsail just enough to remove the horizontal wrinkles from the sail when the boat is beating to windward. We've all seen boats sailing with big scallops between the hanks on their headsail. Don't make the opposite mistake of applying too much halyard tension and causing vertical creases to appear along the luff. This will pull the location of the maximum draft (the deepest point in the curve of the sail) to the front part of the headsail, creating an inefficient shape.

Headsails are designed to carry the maximum draft near the middle of the sail or perhaps just a bit forward of the center. A little experimentation with the halyard will help you determine the proper tension for the wind conditions you are experiencing. When you find the right halyard setting, mark the halyard and a corresponding point on the deck or coaming so that setting is easily replicated. As the wind builds, you'll need more halyard tension to maintain the proper draft location, and if the wind dies, you will have to ease the halyard a bit to regain the correct shape.

Jib-lead adjustment.   While the halyard controls the shape of the luff of the sail and the draft's location, the jibsheet and the jib car or fairlead control the shape of the two other sides, the leech and the foot. If you position the fairlead too far forward, the lower section of the headsail will become round and the leech will get too tight. Sliding the fairlead too far back will have the opposite effect, flattening the foot and causing the leech to twist off to leeward.

Use three pairs of telltales along the luff of your headsail to help you determine the correct position for your jib leads. For each pair of telltales, place one telltale on each side of the sail. One pair should go one third of the way up from the bottom, one in the middle, and one a third of the way down from the top of the sail, all about 9 inches back from the luff. Telltales are easier to read when the ones on the starboard side are placed higher or lower than the ones on the port side. Using a different color on each side of the sail will also help.

It's easiest to set the leads while sailing the boat to weather. As you steer the boat gradually closer to the wind, eventually luffing the headsail, watch the telltales to see which part of the sail begins to luff first. If the lower telltales break before the top ones, the lower sections of the sail are too full. Slide the jib lead back until the telltales break evenly up and down the luff. If the top telltales break first, move the lead forward.

Tacking and gybing. The mechanics of sailing with a jib come into play when it's time to tack or gybe the boat. The lazy jibsheet (the one not in use) should always be prepared for use. Put two wraps of the lazy jibsheet on the winch and pull any slack out of the sheet.

Just before the helmsman begins to tack the boat, make sure there are a minimal number of jibsheet wraps on the active winch – two is usually enough on small boats. As the helmsman turns the boat and the headsail begins to luff, the headsail trimmer should release the jibsheet by pulling it straight up off the winch drum. In very light wind, delaying the release for just a moment, to let the headsail backwind a bit, helps push the bow around.

Once the bow has gone through the eye of the wind, the trimmer should rapidly pull on the new active jibsheet as the sail passes through the foretriangle, created by the headstay, mast, and deck. The last inches of sheet, however, should come in more slowly.

Keeping the sail eased immediately after the tack provides the power the boat needs to build up speed that was lost during the tack. It also gives the trimmer a chance to add wraps on the winch for final trimming. Once the boat is up to speed, trim in the final inches of sheet as the helmsman brings the boat hard on the wind.

The procedure is a bit different when you're gybing the boat. During the gybe, the trimmer should work more closely with the helmsman, easing the sheet slowly as the boat turns away from the wind. This ensures that the jib is working as long as possible and providing power to keep the boat from losing speed during the gybe.

When the boat approaches dead downwind, the jib will be blanketed by the mainsail, so the trimmer can cast the old sheet off the winch and begin trimming the new sheet. After the sail passes through the foretriangle, trim it according to the helmsman's actions.

Communication between the helmsman and the jib trimmer is key during gybes. Skillful trimmers can keep the jib pulling through most of the gybe so the boat loses very little speed.

Overrides. Anytime you are tacking or gybing, there is a chance of getting an override of the sheet on the winch. An override occurs on the winch when one jibsheet wrap jumps up and over a wrap above it. The jibsheet becomes fouled and cannot be eased. Generally, overrides are caused by having too many wraps around the winch. When you're pulling in the jibsheet very fast after a tack and the wraps get loose, they can jump on top of each other. When the sail fills, you have an override. Starting with two wraps and pulling up slightly on the jibsheet as you overhaul it after a tack is the simplest and best way to avoid getting an override.

The problem can be further minimized by placing a turning block between the winch and the headsail's fairlead block to lower the sheet's lead to the winch. Pads under winches can also improve the jibsheet angle. Shape the pad to lead the sheet onto the bottom of the winch drum from an angle slightly greater than perpendicular to the drum.

Adhering to the best precautionary ideas does not prevent overrides altogether, and they are frequently very difficult to remove unless you are able to take the load off the sheet. Luffing the boat head-to-wind may unload the sheet enough to clear it. However, the best way to reduce the load on the fouled sheet is to lead a spare sheet through a jib lead placed right behind or in front of the one in use, if possible, and tie it to the clew grommet of the sail. Then trim it in with a secondary winch or across the cockpit to the other primary winch. With the load on this temporary sheet, it should be easy to clean up the override and return the load to the original sheet.

When all else fails, a sharp knife will solve an override problem every time. If you want to remain on the same tack, rig a secondary sheet. If you want to tack, cut the sheet as the sail begins to luff; then pull in the new active sheet. The helmsman needs to watch the operation closely in case the knife isn't sharp enough and getting through the sheet is taking a long time. If this is the case, slowing the tack a bit should allow ample time to cut the sheet.

Eventually, handling the headsail becomes second nature, akin to riding a bicycle. If the proper precautions are taken, doing it right becomes an art. More important, it can dramatically increase the enjoyment you get from sailing.

Trimming the Genoa for Speed

The power sail always needs some tender loving care

Mike Toppa

The genoa is the most important sail on the boat. Whether it's blowing 5 knots or 25, this is the sail undisturbed wind reaches first and the one on which it has the greatest effect. The mainsail lives in the backwash of the genoa; the headsail is the power generator for boat speed.

The difference between a fast genoa and a slow one is its shape. You wouldn't think of getting on an airplane if you saw the fat part of the wing in the back. Similarly, you can't hope to go fast on a boat with misshaped sails.

Today, because of widespread use of low-stretch materials like Kevlar and Mylar, the shape built into the sail won't change much during use. While every sailmaker uses a particular panel orientation to limit stretch, the original sail shape is what counts – and achieving the designed genoa shape makes the difference between going fast or dogging it.

Most boats have different size genoas for different wind strengths. Rating rules determine the maximum size, and the biggest sails are used in lighter winds until the boat reaches its stability limit. As wind increases, the bigger sails overpower the boat and drag overcomes the lift produced, so a smaller sail is needed.

You have onboard controls that affect the shape of the genoa; knowing how to use them will increase all-around performance and get you to the finish line sooner. Even if you've bought the world's fastest genoa shapes from your sailmaker, it's still up to you to make them perform. You must first decide which size sail is appropriate. Your boat's stability and the amount of crew weight you carry will determine the maximum wind strength for your biggest genoa. Normally you start reducing headsail area when the boat's heel angle exceeds 23 degrees or the wind gets up to about 20 knots true. From 20 to 25 knots, the #2 genoa is most efficient. In higher winds, use the #3.

Once you have hoisted the genoa, the halyard should be tensioned so the sail's maximum draft is about 45 percent of the total girth distance back from the luff. Low-stretch materials enable sail shape to be built reliably into the sail, with the draft located where it should be. For this reason, the halyard should be used more to hold the genoa up in the air than to force the draft forward in the sail.

When you're using a new Mylar or Kevlar genoa, be sure not to overtension the halyard. In most cases, bring it up *hand tight,* and then take a look at the draft location. If the sail is properly designed, this halyard setting should be very close to correct. You may see wrinkles or creases along the luff in lighter air, but it's the draft location in the sail that's important. As the wind increases, you may have to increase luff tension with the halyard to keep the draft forward, but this adjustment should be very minor.

In flat water you can set the halyard at minimum tension to keep the draft at 45 percent and the luff as flat and as straight as possible. This shape allows you to point higher because the angle of attack of the wind to the sail is at a minimum. In waves or difficult steering conditions, however, you want to shape the genoa so the entry is rounder and the draft is a bit farther forward. The rounder entry creates a wider angle of attack; even though you won't be able to feather the boat quite so high into the wind, the wider angle of attack makes the boat easier to steer and is more forgiving.

The next step is to adjust the fore-and-aft lead on the deck to set up the desired leech twist and vertical profile. Because of wind sheer – the difference between the wind angle at deck level and the wind angle at the top of the sail – the leech must be twisted off to match this difference in wind angles.

The correct fore-and-aft lead for a genoa varies from one day to the next, depending on the wind sheer. The more wind sheer there is, the more twist you need in the sail. You should mark the *average* lead setting for your genoa on the deck. Before every race, though, take a good look at the sail; you may want to change the lead for the day's race in response to the wind sheer.

Telltales on the genoa luff also help tell you if the twist is correct. Too much twist causes the upper telltales to luff before the bottom ones. If this is the case, try moving the lead forward. Too little twist, with the lead placed too far forward, makes the bottom section of the genoa too full, and the sail will luff here first. Move the lead back until the sail luffs evenly from top to bottom. The vertical profile of the sail should be aligned so the leech is the same distance from the upper spreader or shroud as the foot is from the shroud base. That's a good starting point for lead adjustment, but always check the settings against boat speed.

Twist adjustment is needed when the wind increases and you become overpowered. You depower the genoa by moving the lead back and twisting off the top of the sail. The top of the sail opens up, making it less efficient, and the bottom quarter of the genoa is pulled tighter and flattened out. The end result is a flatter sail working at 80 percent of its efficiency. This technique provides a good safety valve until you can change to a smaller sail.

Another genoa control is headstay tension, which controls the depth of the genoa. Imagine a genoa attached to the boat by the tack, the halyard at the masthead, and the clew. If the backstay is eased, the headstay sags; this makes the sail fuller. The more tension you apply to the headstay, using the permanent backstay on a masthead rig or the runners on a fractional sail plan, the less the headstay will sag. Headstay sag has an effect the opposite of that which mast bend has on the main. When you straighten the mast, the mainsail gets fuller. When you straighten the headstay, the genoa becomes flatter.

Determining the correct amount of depth of a genoa depends on the conditions, your boat's stability, and the tactical situation. I think of the depth adjustment in the sail as the boat's accelerator and gear shift. In power situations, when you need maximum speed – going off the starting line, for example, or when you want to roll over a boat that just tacked on your lee bow – you want to have a fuller setting. These are the times when you need to step on the gas. Ease the backstay and sheet in the genoa to make the headsail shape fuller. You can gain as much as 5 percent in boat speed. Even though velocity made good to windward won't be 100 percent, you'll have the extra speed you need to get your bow out in front of the competition.

The same situation applies when you are sailing in waves and generally sloppy conditions. A strong wind that's been blowing for some time will generate waves that slow you down. Similarly, in the light air after a hard blow, there are leftover waves that stop the boat. This is when you need a fuller than normal setting to power up the genoa to keep the boat moving at top speed.

Once the genoa is set up for the prevailing conditions, the sheet becomes the most important control. It's hard to describe exact sheet tension for all boats because spreader lengths and sheeting angles vary from boat to boat. Some general rules apply:

- Trimming in the sheet flattens the sail and reduces twist. It allows you to point higher, but it also reduces the chord depth, which reduces power.
- Easing out the sheet makes the sail fuller and more powerful. It reduces your pointing ability but increases boat speed.

Sheet tension should be changed with every change in wind velocity and direction. When a puff hits, the sail does stretch some and get fuller. To compensate, trim in the sheet to counteract the change and maintain the basic design shape. If you "sail into a hole" and wind velocity decreases, the genoa becomes less pressurized and flatter. In this situation, you should ease out the sheet to make the sail fuller and maintain speed through the water.

Sailing in shifty conditions requires constant changes in sheet tension because many times the helmsman can't react fast enough to these changes. For example, if you sail into a big lift, the jib will become stalled before the helmsman has a chance to steer up into the wind; he or she simply can't turn the boat fast enough. This is when the jibsheet should be eased out to respond to the new wind direction and then slowly retrimmed as the boat comes up onto the wind. Boat speed increases concurrently, so the genoa can be trimmed very tight as the boat heads up to burn off that extra burst of speed and to point higher.

Conversely, if you sail into a header, the jib will luff, and the boat will slow down. Now the helmsman has to head off to adjust to the new wind direction. The trimmer should pull the sheet in hard when the jib luffs and then ease it back out to a speed-building setting as the boat starts to head down. Once boat speed is back to normal, the sail can be trimmed in to the normal setting.

Sailing through oncoming waves requires the same kind of sheet-tensioning adjustments. To keep the boat moving, the helmsman should head up going up the front of a wave, and fall off going down its back. The trimmer has to adjust the sails constantly to meet these changing apparent-wind angles.

The hardest condition for the jib trimmer is when the boat is sailing upwind, while a swell left over from some previous wind condition is coming up from astern. The waves hitting the stern sections of the boat increase boat speed, and apparent wind changes constantly as a result. The helmsman must use the helm much more in these conditions, and the jib must be trimmed in and out continuously to maintain the basic trim setting.

The only efficient way to keep the jib correctly trimmed for these changes is to maintain constant communication between the helmsman and the trimmer. To enhance communication on some 12-meter boats, deck layouts have been changed so the steering wheels are farther forward and as close as possible to the jib trimmers.

The genoa trimmer must continually change the setting and the trim for every change in wind, wave, and steering conditions. If you can work your boat through the ever-present wind shifts and the continuously changing motion of the waves, you should be able to sail past a good part of the fleet – certainly past all those who are not trimming their sails as aggressively as you are. If you are the trimmer, keep your eyes on the shape of the sail, keep talking to the helmsman, and try hard to adjust the sheet to every new bit of wind and waves that comes your way.

Controlling the Mainsail

The mainsail is the main attraction

Roger Marshall

In this day of the big genoa headsail, we tend to forget that the mainsail is just as important to winning a race or enjoying a cruise or a day sail. It is not just the genoa that does the work. When you are sailing to windward, you can adjust the mainsail to ease the pressure on the helm and significantly increase your boat speed. And by easing the traveler when a puff hits, the mainsail can balance off the potential for increased heel angle.

But to get the most out of your mainsail, you must know when and how to use all its controls: the main halyard and the cunningham for adjusting luff tension, the outhaul for tensioning the foot, the mainsheet for positioning the boom and tensioning the leech, the vang and flattening reef for adjusting leech tension, and the traveler for controlling the sail's angle of attack.

If you have a genoa on your boat, for best results the mainsail leech should be approximately parallel to that of the genoa. To understand why, imagine that you are sailing to windward with just your mainsail. Aerodynamics tell us that the mast will disrupt the flow of air over the sail. Even though the invisible streamlines moving on the weather side tend to straighten, those on the leeward side remain turbulent until they reattach to the sail about two-thirds of the way back from the leading edge.

Suppose you place a genoa in front of the mainsail. The overflow now passes through a slot between the two sails, which helps reduce the turbulence on the leeward side of the main. Therefore, when the shape of the main conforms to the shape of the genoa, the airflow through the slot will be fairly constant from top to bottom. As a result, both sails will be

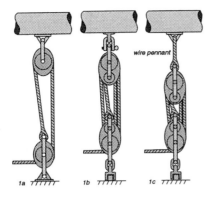

wire pennant

1a   1b   1c

Fig. 1 *Two- and four-part mainsheet configurations are standard for many trimming situations.*

approaching their maximum efficiency.

The mainsheet, traveler, and vang can do a great deal to keep the mainsail shape similar to that of the genoa. We'll take a look at what each one does and how it might be adjusted to work best under different sailing conditions.

Mainsheet. Mainsheet rigs come in various shapes and sizes. Figures 1a and 1b show simple two- and four-part mainsheets which can either be led to a winch or pulled in by hand. But they create windage which can be reduced by using a wire pennant to lower the height of the top block (Fig. 1c). All these mainsheet arrangements are extremely efficient either when they are used with a traveler and taglines to control athwartships movement or when they are linked to a single fixed point on the deck.

These mainsheet arrangements do have one disadvantage when they are used with a traveler. The block that leads to the winch must be positioned on the centerline, which causes the boom to be pulled toward the center of the boat when the boom is under load. You can remedy this by leading the mainsheet forward (Fig. 2). The additional blocks, however, do create some extra friction and make the sail slower to trim.

Many other mainsheet systems are possible, but most of them just complicate matters more. The layout shown in Figure 3, for example, may look efficient, but all the blocks must turn when the traveler is moved. Under load, this is often next to impossible. I believe that a single-part tackle that is led to a powerful winch is the simplest and most efficient method of trimming a mainsheet. And if a rope sheet is fitted, a self-tailing winch makes the trimming job even easier.

Whatever the final design of your mainsheet lead system, its major function is to help shape the sail. Mainsheet tension is critical - too little tension allows the sail to twist off at the top, while too much tension can pull the leech up straight and stall the airflow out of the sail. Boat speed decreases in both cases. The mainsheet is set properly when the telltales are streaming aft. The telltales should be sewn into each batten pocket with one or two more sewn forward in the belly of the sail.

The precise amount of mainsheet tension varies from boat to boat, and a lot depends upon the mast's bending characteristics and the cut of the sail. For example, some sailmakers build racing mainsails with a very large roach to gain extra unmeasured sail area and to increase efficiency by having more of the sail aft of the airflow reattachment point. The trouble is that these large roaches are notoriously hard to control and require considerable mainsheet tension, even in light air. A large roach also requires careful mainsheet positioning. When the mainsheet is attached to the end of the boom, the mainsheet pulls down vertically and tensioning the leech of the sail is much easier. Contrast this with a situation where the sheet is attached to the middle of the boom, or when it is led aft. With this arrangement, controlling the leech by mainsheet alone is far more difficult (Fig. 4).

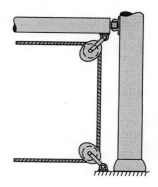

Fig. 2 *To avoid pulling the boom toward centerline, while trimming, lead the mainsheet to the forward end of the boom, then bring it down to a winch.*

You should recheck the position of the mainsheet on your own boat to see if you can change it to get improved efficiency or leverage.

Traveler. Positioning a boom is much easier if the lower block of the mainsheet is attached to a traveler that moves athwartships along a track. The track itself should be long enough to allow you to take the traveler well to windward in light air and well to leeward in heavy air. On many boats, the traveler is set in a fixed position by adjustable stops. While these stops are satisfactory, in many situations the traveler is often difficult to adjust precisely and obviously cannot provide totally accurate trim control. A better racing arrangement uses taglines (traveler control lines) for quick adjustment which are typically set up with one or two parts.

While the mainsheet helps you obtain the best possible sail shape, the traveler helps you set your sail at the optimum angle to the wind. To find your ideal angle of attack, you first watch the knotmeter, helm, and heel angles, and then adjust the traveler and mainsheet accordingly. When the traveler is pulled too far to windward, both the helm and heel angle will increase, and the boat should begin to slow. When you ease the traveler out too much, the sail will start to luff, the helm and heel angles will decrease, and boat speed will also drop.

In addition to these routine adjustments, give some attention to the traveler under special kinds of weather conditions. In a sloppy sea, for

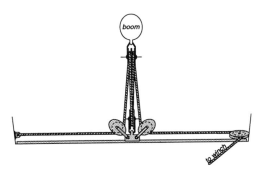

Fig. 3 *The traveler arrangement shown here looks efficient but because all of the blocks must turn when the traveler is adjusted, friction builds up under load.*

example, the traveler should be eased a bit more than usual to produce needed extra drive from the mainsail. When you are sailing in gusty winds, you can slide the traveler down to leeward to reduce the boat's heel angle in a gust, and then pull it back to its original position after the wind speed has dropped. Doing this does not affect the basic shape of the sail.

Vang. If the boom is eased out beyond the outboard end of the traveler, it must be held down by a vang, and also held forward by a preventer. A vang can be rope, adjustable steel bar, or hydraulic; it depends on how versatile you want the system to be.

A rope vang is usually a three- or five-part tackle similar to the mainsheet system. You can attach it with the inboard end at the mast, or you might run it on a circular track. A circular track arrangement is more efficient because the pull of the vang is always straight down from its attachment point on the boom. An adjustable steel bar or hydraulic vang has the advantage of actually supporting the boom in addition to adjusting the mainsail. But a steel bar vang is slower to operate and adds some extra

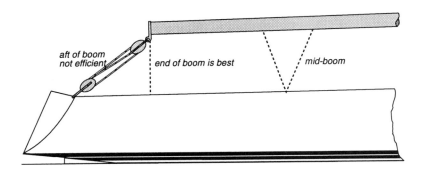

Fig. 4 *If the mainsheet is the primary control for leech tension, end of the boom positioning is best.*

weight above deck. A hydraulic vang is almost always attached at a single point, usually to the mast and as near as possible to the deck. Its great advantage is that it is easy to use and allows for a very precise adjustment, but it does require a hydraulic pump system.

The vang has always been thought of as a device just to tension the leech of the mainsail, but it has many more uses. I've mentioned that a bar or hydraulic vang can also support the boom, and on smaller boats it can bend the mast or boom to help flatten the main. Figure 5 illustrates the mechanics of such a system in simple terms. One well-known use for the vang is to prevent the boom from rising during a gybe. For example, if the mainsail were allowed to swing across without a vang and without someone pulling the sheet in during a gybe, the boom could rise up high enough so that it could hit the backstay. If this happened, either the boom or the backstay might be broken. Older boats with longer booms use a vang to stop the boom from bending upward and making the mainsail fuller than it ought to be.

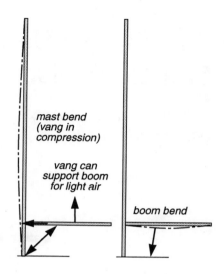

mast bend (vang in compression)

vang can support boom for light air

boom bend

Fig 5 *The boom vang is primarily used to control mainsail leech tension. On some smaller boats, the boom vang can be used to bend the mast and boom to flatten the main.*

The mainsheet, traveler, and vang must be used together to create good mainsail shape and to get the sail aligned to the wind at the best possible angle. There are other mainsail controls, but these three are the ones that a mainsail trimmer needs to adjust most often. And that is why they are also the ones that will make the most difference to the speed of your boat, no matter whether you are cruising or on the race course.

Sail Shape: Using Sail Controls

Additional gear can lead to better performance

Jeff Johnstone

Sailmakers design sails for the average boat with a general shape in mind. In order to make the boat perform well in any wind speed, the sails must first be trimmed for the wind direction and course and then shaped so they are drawing well. Shaping the sails is the function of certain mechanical devices - the sail controls. The skipper's job is to use them correctly to keep the boat performing efficiently under all conditions, especially when going upwind.

When your boat is heeling excessively in a breeze and wants to round up, your sails are generating too much power - the boat is said to be *overpowered*. On the other hand, if you are sailing in light to moderate winds and the boat is standing upright and going slowly, the boat is probably *underpowered*. Your goal when sailing upwind is to use the sail controls to *depower* (keep the boat from being overwhelmed by the wind) or *power up* (use the wind to maintain boat speed).

A sail is powered up when it has a full shape (lots of curve) and a closed leech (top batten parallel to the boom). A depowered sail is flat, with an open leech (angled to leeward). Let's look at the gear that controls sail shape.

Mainsail controls. The *halyard* primarily hoists the sail, but its tightness affects the draft position (fore-and-aft point of maximum depth in the sail) and the leech tension. A tight halyard pulls the draft forward and opens (slackens) the leech. A loose halyard closes (tightens) the leech and moves the draft aft.

In most conditions, you should tighten the halyard to remove horizontal wrinkles in the mainsail, but do not pull so hard that you induce vertical stress wrinkles along the luff. Never adjust the halyard when the sail in under full load; you risk breaking a halyard shackle. Be sure to release other controls (mainsheet, boom vang, and cunningham) when you are adjusting the main halyard in order to relieve the pressure on the sail.

The *outhaul* pulls the foot of the sail along the boom, affecting the fullness of the lower part of the sail. Tightening the outhaul stretches the foot and flattens the sail; loosening the outhaul bags up the lower part of the main. Like the main halyard, the outhaul is easiest to adjust when the mainsail is not under full load.

In almost all conditions, except light to moderate air with choppy seas, keep the outhaul tight enough to maintain a horizontal stress wrinkle that is on the verge of showing along the foot. When in doubt, set the outhaul tight before hoisting the sail. It's always easier to release the outhaul than to trim it in.

The *mainsheet* is the most versatile mainsail control. It not only controls the angle of the sail to the wind, but it also affects the fullness and leech tension. You can sail upwind in 20 knots with a baggy main and still be fast if the mainsheet is handled properly.

As you trim the mainsheet, the boom is pulled laterally toward the centerline. The closer to the centerline the boom comes, the more the mainsheet begins to pull down on the boom, which in turn pulls down on the leech. With enough tension, especially on smaller boats, a tight mainsheet will bend the mast and stretch or flatten the sail.

In winds up to 12 knots, trim the mainsheet until the top batten is parallel to the boom. (To help you see the position of the batten, place a strip of dark tape on the batten pocket.) In stronger winds, when the boat is overpowered and becomes difficult to keep at a steady angle of heel, ease out the mainsheet. In puffy conditions, combine easing the sheet with steering the boat a few degrees closer to the wind. Then, as the puff subsides, bear away a few degrees and trim the main back in. This subtle upwind slalom course should keep the boat at a constant angle of heel, making it more efficient and comfortable to sail.

The halyard, outhaul, and mainsheet are the basic mainsail controls. More speed and fun can be had by using four additional devices: backstay, cunningham, traveler, and boom vang.

The *backstay*, which runs between the masthead and transom of the boat, supports the mast. Sometimes the lower end of the backstay is split into two wires going to the outer quarters of the transom; a block-and-tackle attached to a ring and sliders on the wires can be used to put tension on the stay. There are also various mechanical and hydraulic means of doing the same job. The backstay directly affects the fullness, draft position, and leech tension of the mainsail. Tightening the backstay depowers the sail by pulling the top of the mast aft and bowing the middle of the mast forward. The bowed mast pulls sailcloth out of the front of the main, thereby flattening the shape, moving the draft aft, and opening the leech.

The *cunningham* is a line or a small block-and-tackle that runs from the first grommet above the gooseneck on the luff of the sail to the base of the mast. Tightening it pulls down on the lower luff of the sail and moves the draft position. The cunningham usually is adjusted to keep the draft in the middle of the sail. If you depower the main by tightening the backstay, remember to counteract the aft movement of the draft by pulling on the cunningham; the cunningham and backstay are always tightened and loosened together. If your boat is not equipped with an adjustable backstay, you will still need to tighten the cunningham as the wind builds because the tension from the other controls, especially the mainsheet, will push the draft aft.

The mainsheet block attaches to the *traveler*, a sliding car on a track placed athwart the cockpit or cabin roof; it controls the inboard/outboard position of the boom in relation to the centerline. In winds under 12 knots, set the mainsheet so that the top batten is parallel to the boom and then pull the traveler to windward until the boom is on the centerline of the boat. In stronger winds, you can either keep the traveler centered and ease the mainsheet or cleat the mainsheet and ease the traveler. In puffy conditions, it is usually safer to center the traveler and adjust the mainsheet because the mainsheet has a greater range of movement and can balance the boat even in heavy gusts.

The *boom vang* is a block-and-tackle or hydraulic device that runs from a point one-third of the way along the inboard end of the boom to the base of the mast. Many sailors use the vang only as a downwind control to keep the boom from rising. But it can also be used effectively upwind, especially in breezier conditions. In a 15-knot breeze, if you ease the mainsheet with the boom vang slack, the boom not only moves to leeward but up as well, opening the leech too much and ruining the airfoil shape you spent so much time to create. At this point, the mainsail has no power and the boat develops lee helm (the tendency for the boat to bear off).

Your goal is to balance the boat (to have a slight weather helm) but still have enough power to sail fast and point close to the wind. Keep the leech firm by tensioning the boom vang while at the same time angling the leech to leeward by easing the mainsheet. The firm leech gives the sail power and pointing ability, while angling it to leeward keeps the boat balanced. In winds under 12 knots, keep the boom vang slack and use the mainsheet to control leech tension.

Jib controls.   As the jib is supported only at its leading edge, its shape can be radically modified by sail controls. Unless your jib is rigged with a cunningham, *jib halyard* adjustment primarily controls the draft of the sail. A tight halyard stretches the luff and pulls the draft forward, while a slack halyard moves the draft aft.

For most conditions, tension the halyard so that horizontal wrinkles at the luff are on the verge of showing. In a well-designed sail, this sets the draft at approximately one-third aft. In windy conditions with big waves, pull the halyard tight. This action will move the draft forward, creating a more rounded sail entry that in turn enables the helmsman to steer through a wider course range without stalling the sail (wind does not flow around both sides of the sail).

The *jib-lead position* is the fore-and-aft and inboard/outboard angle at which the jibsheet is trimmed through a sliding *jib block* located on a track on the side deck. To determine the proper fore-and-aft location of the block, slowly turn the boat into the wind and watch the luff of the jib. If the jib luffs first at the top, it means that the jibsheet is pulling the lower part of the sail more tightly than the upper part, indicating that the jib lead is too far aft. If the jib luffs low first, then the lead is too far forward.

For winds up to 12 knots, set the lead blocks so that the jib luffs evenly from bottom to top. As the breeze increases, slide the blocks aft so that the bottom of the sail can be pulled flat while the top of the sail spills wind. Mark the jib lead positions so you can locate them easily.

For most sailing, the jib leads are positioned on standard inboard tracks. However, if your boat has outboard tracks or toerails that will accommodate snatch blocks, you can take advantage of *outboard sheeting* - running the sheets through blocks attached to the toerail. Outboard sheeting is most effective in lots of wind and big seas, when you want to widen the slot between the main and jib and let the wind escape.

Of all the controls, the *jibsheet* has the greatest effect on the jib. As the sheet is trimmed in, the sail moves inboard, the leech tightens and the shape flattens. With a little experimenting, you can make your jib look as full as a paper sack or as flat as a board. Once the halyard and jib leads are set for the conditions, trim in the sheet until the leech of the jib parallels that of the main. You'll know the sheet is trimmed in too much if you see a backwind "bubble" in the luff of the main or the helmsman complains that the boat is difficult to steer. If you are sailing with a larger jib (genoa) that overlaps the main, use the distance of the sail off the spreader tip (it should not be touching) as a reference for trim.

Remember that as the wind velocity changes, so must your jibsheet. As the wind increases, the sail stretches to leeward and must be trimmed to the proper position. If you sail into a calm spot, ease out the sheet to maintain speed. In very windy conditions, with the halyard tight and the jib lead aft, leave the sheet eased a few inches to keep the boat balanced.

Remember, too, that you can sail well by simply adjusting the main halyard, outhaul and mainsheet, jib halyard, jib leads, and jibsheet. The other sail controls are for fine-tuning. When you use them correctly, you'll have the pleasure of knowing that you are sailing to the maximum of the boat's ability - and your own.

Telltales for Fast Trim

Little additions can have a big effect

Dave Franzel

Nothing you can do for your boat provides as much accurate and reliable information per penny spent as telltales. For the price of a pack of gum, you can rig telltales for your mainsail and jib that can help you sail your boat more efficiently and faster.

There are two different applications for telltales. Tied to a shroud or backstay, they flow in the direction of the apparent wind. Knowing the apparent-wind angle helps you trim your sails on all points of sail. Sewn or taped to the leech of the mainsail and along the jib's luff, telltales provide an enormous amount of information about the airflow across your sails. This information allows you to steer an excellent close-hauled course and, more important, lets you trim your sails with great accuracy. The most useful locations for telltales on your sails are on the leech of the mainsail at each batten pocket and at three evenly spaced locations along the jib's luff, about eight inches aft of the forestay.

If you prefer yarn, use the tightly wound, oily variety because it sheds water. Pass the end of a six-foot length of yarn through a sailmaker's needle (a small loop of thread or whipping twine can be passed through the eye and used to pull the yarn through). Then tie a stopper knot in the end of the yarn and pass the needle through the aft end of a batten pocket in the mainsail. Be careful not to go through the leech line, if your sail has one. Cut the yarn about six inches from the sail. You still have five-plus feet of yarn already led through the needle, so tie another stopper knot in the end and pass the needle through the next batten pocket, and so on.

For jib-luff telltales, tie a stopper knot six inches from the end of the yarn, pass the needle through the sail, and pull to the knot. Tie a knot just on the other side of the sail and cut the yarn at six inches.

Audio-cassette tape and prepackaged telltales made of ripstop nylon work as well, although the cassette tape may be a little too sensitive. Tape one end of the telltale with small circles of ripstop sail tape, or use the adhesive circles provided in the kits. The sail must be absolutely clean and dry for the tape to stick on any kind of permanent basis. Tape the star-board-side telltales an inch or two higher than the port, so you can tell which is which when sailing. Using two different colors helps too.

Mainsail leech telltales.   Telltales on the main's leech, particularly the one at the top batten, are the primary guides for judging mainsheet tension and therefore mainsail trim. When sailing close-hauled, trim the mainsail until the telltales stream straight aft to indicate a smooth, attached airflow along the entire curve of the sail. This is the "go-fast" mode of sail-ing, but you sacrifice some pointing ability.

For maximum pointing ability, trim the main a little tighter, until the top batten's telltale is "stalled," or not streaming aft. The stalled telltale shows that the airflow does not remain attached along the entire curve of the sail. In this mode you can point high, but straight-line speed is compro-mised. For most boats sailing close-hauled in relatively flat water, the most efficient trim is achieved when the top batten's telltale streams about half the time and is stalled half the time.

When reaching, trim the main and the boom vang so the telltales on the leech stream aft all the time for maximum speed. First ease the sheet until the main just starts to luff, and then trim it in a little. Next, tension the boom vang until the telltales start to stall, and then ease it a little to keep all the telltales streaming.

Jib-luff telltales.   When your jib is trimmed correctly for sailing close-hauled in most conditions, all the jib's telltales will stream aft. Also, if you head up slightly from a close-hauled course, all three windward telltales will become turbulent, or lift, simultaneously, indicating that there is a per-fect airflow at all points along the luff. If the top telltale lifts first, there is too much twist in the sail. Move the jib's fairlead or block forward to bring in the top of the sail more and decrease the twist. If the bottom telltale lifts first, move the lead aft.

If the windward telltales lift when the jib leads are in the right place, the air is not flowing smoothly on the windward side of the sail. Steer away from the wind, head off a little, or trim the sail in if you can until the tell-tales stream aft. If the leeward telltales are turbulent, the sail is stalled.

Ease the sail or steer closer to the wind. When both windward and leeward telltales are flowing straight aft, it's a beautiful thing – and indicates a good close-hauled course.

It is worthwhile experimenting with telltales in other locations. For example, try a set in the center of the mainsail one-quarter of the way down from the head, to investigate airflow there. But don't overdo it. If Persian rugs were fast, sails would look very different than they do today.

Getting Out of Irons

It's embarrassing, but nothing
to worry about

John Alofsin

Sailors – both experienced and novice – can get stopped head-to-wind or what is commonly called "in irons." Armed with just a little information, you can get yourself out of irons and on your way quickly and reliably.

Since a boat cannot sail directly into the wind, a boat held in the head-to-wind position will quickly slow down and lose steerage. A boat is in irons when it is stopped with the wind dead ahead.

Poorly executed tacks are the most common cause of getting stuck in irons. If a boat doesn't have enough speed to carry it through the wind during a tack, it can get stuck in irons. When tacking, be sure to start with plenty of speed and to turn the boat crisply all the way through the wind.

All sailors should know how to get out of irons. The tried-and-true method for boats of all sizes is to back the jib. First decide which tack you want to be on when you get out of irons. Then, with the tiller centered, trim the jib to the opposite side so that the wind will push the boat onto the desired tack.

For example, if you want the bow to go to the right so that you end up on port tack, trim the port jibsheet; this presents a small amount of the jib to the wind. When the wind catches the backed jib, it will push the bow onto port tack. If your boat is small, a crew member can hold the jib out to present more jib area to the wind so that it backs more quickly (Fig. 1). Trim the starboard sheet if you want to end up on starboard tack.

Backwinding the main on small boats with or without jibs is also an effective way to get out of irons. Push the boom about 30 to 40 degrees off

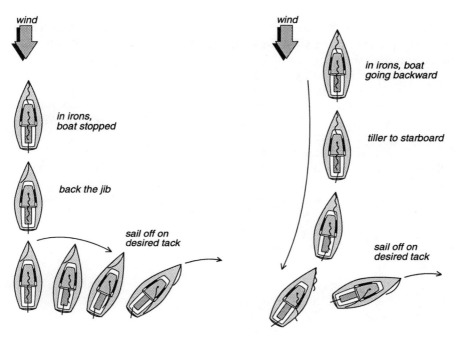

Fig. 1 *The tried-and-true way to get out of irons on a small boat is to have a crew member hold the clew of the jib out on the side of the boat opposite the direction you want to go. The wind will push the bow onto the desired tack, at which time the jib can be trimmed on the proper side.*

Fig. 2 *If the boat begins to move backward while you are in irons, push the tiller in the direction you want the boat to go. To go right, push the tiller to the starboard side of the boat.*

the boat's centerline in the direction opposite the one you want your bow to go. If you want the bow to go to the right (port tack), push the main to port. The main is usually a much bigger sail than the jib and therefore is more difficult to control. Be careful when backing the main, particularly in strong winds. Also, because the main is located near the middle of the boat, its leverage in moving the bow from head-to-wind to either tack is not as great as the jib's. Think of the effect a person's weight has at the end of a seesaw (jib) compared with that at the center of it (main).

With either method, if the boat remains in irons long enough, the wind will begin to push it backward. Once the boat is moving again, even backward, you can use your rudder to steer. Remember, you are going in reverse, so the tiller and rudder work in reverse. If you want the bow to go right (port tack), move the tiller to the right. Once the boat falls onto port tack and the sails fill, you will begin to move forward again, and the tiller and rudder will operate normally. The fastest and most effective way to get out of irons is to back both sails and use the rudder at the same time.

When the boat is out of irons, trim the jib first and then the main to begin moving forward. The jib helps pull the bow away from the wind to prevent getting caught in irons while you are accelerating.

As with any sailing skill, practicing getting out of irons is important. Take some time and intentionally put yourself in irons. This will help you see what causes the problem. Then practice getting out so that when the time comes you can smoothly get your boat back on the tack you want.

Light-Air Sailing

Make the most of a tranquil situation

Barbara Stetson

In moderate wind, the average sailor can determine the exact wind direction and get his or her boat moving. It takes more skill and concentration to be a good light-air sailor. The following pointers can help.

Finding the wind always comes first. A masthead fly is the best wind direction indicator because the sails and rigging interfere less with the wind's flow at the top of the mast. Masthead flies range from a stick with a piece of yarn attached to it to a Windex-style pointer. A piece of yarn at the masthead fly will flow in the same direction as the wind, while a Windex-style masthead fly will point directly toward the wind.

Another good wind indicator is a six-to-eight-inch piece of yarn or cassette tape tied to the shrouds at about shoulder height. This type of wind indicator also flows with the wind.

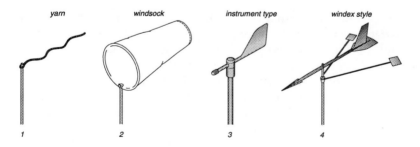

Fig. 1 *There are many types of masthead flies. A few of the more popular models are shown here.*

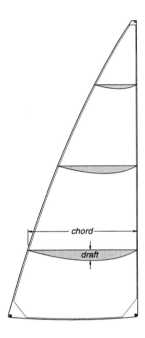

Fig. 2   *The draft of the mainsail is the distance from an imaginary straight line between the leech and the luff to the sail's surface.*

In extremely light wind, when the masthead fly is going around in circles and the shroud telltales are hanging limp, your skin can be the best wind indicator. Wet the top of your pointing finger, then turn it. The palm side of your finger will feel coldest when it faces the wind. Also, when sailing on a reach or downwind, stick your neck out, because you can feel the wind's direction on the back of your neck.

Always be on the lookout for puffs of air, which make ripples on the water. Smoke coming out of smoke stacks, flags on flagpoles, and dark water in the distance can also help you locate a new breeze and its direction. Try to head your boat for the new wind.

Once you know the wind's direction, proper sail trim will get you moving as fast as possible. When sailing close-hauled or reaching, the curvature of the sails is very important to proper trim. In light air you need more curvature, or draft, in the sail. The chord of a sail is an imaginary straight line from the luff to the leech parallel to the boom. The draft is the distance from the chord to the sail's surface.

On most boats the mainsail's draft is adjusted with the outhaul, which controls the tension in the foot of the sail, and the cunningham and halyard, which adjust the tension in the luff. If your boat has a jib, the jib's draft is adjusted with the jibsheet and halyard.

When raising the mainsail, pull the halyard until the horizontal wrinkles extending back from the mast along the luff just barely disappear. Keep the luff tension as low as possible. Ease the outhaul until the sail's deepest draft along the foot is six to ten inches to leeward of the boom.

Sailing upwind.   Once you are sailing, keep the mainsheet as loose as possible and make sure the boom vang, if your boat has one, is eased completely. Telltales along the leech, one at each batten, are the best guides for sheet tension. Trim the mainsheet until the top telltale disappears behind the sail, and then ease the mainsheet until the top telltale just begins to flow off the leech. If the wind is too light to lift the telltales, ease the mainsheet until the end of the boom is above the leeward rail of the boat.

To increase draft in the jib, if you have movable sheet fairleads, move them forward a few inches from their normal position. By moving the fairleads forward, you create more curvature in the foot of the jib. Trim the jibsheet until the foot and leech are equally curved to create a full sail. If your boat is not equipped with movable fairleads, trim the jib according to the telltales. In either case, if there is not enough wind to lift the luff telltales, imagine a straight line between the clew, where the sheets are attached, and the tack, the bottom forward corner of the sail, and trim the sail until this line is parallel to the boom.

To fill the sails in light air, heel the boat about 15 degrees by having the crew sit to leeward. Position the crew so that the leeward topside is most submerged at a point halfway between the bow and the stern. Gravity will then pull the sails into the shape of a curve.

Once you have found the wind and have trimmed the sails properly, the next objective is to get your boat moving. Do not sail too close to the wind. Sail a close reach, about 60 degrees off the wind. In light air it's more important to get the boat moving than to point as close to the wind as possible. The boat will stall if you point too close to the wind. To reduce drag through the water, keep the rudder as straight as possible, turning it only when necessary.

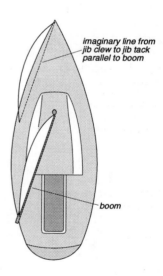

imaginary line from jib clew to jib tack parallel to boom

boom

In very light air you will not feel the boat's forward speed. Judge forward movement by watching for bubbles passing by or a slight wake behind the boat.

Sailing downwind. In very light winds, don't sail directly with the wind. The fastest course to your downwind destination is a broad reach. Steer the boat onto a broad reach, and then set your sails perpendicular to the wind. Have the crew sit to leeward, as you did when sailing upwind, and again keep rudder movement to a minimum.

If you have a spinnaker, it can increase your boat speed by increasing sail area. While sailing on a broad reach, set the spinnaker pole perpendicular to the wind, as you normally would. If there is enough wind to

Fig. 3 *While sailing upwind when there isn't enough wind to make the telltales fly, trim the main so the boom is over the leeward rail and trim the jib so an imaginary line from the jib's clew to its tack parallels the boom.*

even partially fill the spinnaker, lower the pole until the clews are at the same level. This keeps the spinnaker symmetrical and as easy as possible to fly.

If the spinnaker will not fill on a broad reach, head up closer to the wind to a beam reach. You won't be sailing toward your destination, but the most important thing is to get the sail filled. Once it fills, head down toward a broad reach. If it starts to collapse, head back up to a beam reach again. This S-shaped course is the fastest course to your destination. Try not to get discouraged when the spinnaker does not fill, because you will still be going faster than you would be without it.

Current effect. Current will have a greater effect on your course in light air than it will in moderate or heavy air. Since the boat's speed is so slow, the current can push the boat sideways, forward, or even backward. Look at buoys, lobster- or crab-pot markers, anchored boats, or any other stationary objects near you to determine the direction and strength of the current. These objects will create turbulence on the water's surface on their down-current side. The more turbulent the wake, the stronger the current. If you sail on a river, the current will push you downstream. In light air it is better to sail upstream first, and then return by sailing downstream.

Even when the leaves are still and the water is flat, there's usually a bit of breeze to get moving. With skills and knowledge, sailing in light air can be relaxing and fun.

Safe Sailing Downwind

*Knowing a few tricks can keep you
out of trouble*

Scott Rohrer

Sailing downwind seems to be the easy way to sail. The boat is upright, and clothes and bodies can warm up and dry out. It's also the easiest angle of sail to understand – the wind pushes you along, employing no wonders of physics. For centuries this was the only way to sail. Even today there remains a school of thought that "gentlemen don't sail to windward."

Safe and easy downwind sailing requires certain techniques in both sail trim and helmsmanship. When the wind is blowing exactly in the direction you want to go, your point of sail is "dead downwind," and you can set the sails on either side of the boat (Photo 1). But you should realize that on this point of sail, the sails may want to change sides, or gybe, without much warning for you or the crew.

Sail trim.   When the wind is blowing from directly behind you, the sails are stalled and won't luff, regardless of their angle. Trim the mainsail so that the boom is roughly perpendicular to the wind direction; the belly of the sail will press against the leeward shrouds. Look at your masthead fly or a shroud telltale to determine the wind direction.

You'll soon notice that the boom rises and the sail twists off at the top when the boom is out this far. This is inefficient at best and increases rolling and the possibility of gybing. Rig a boom vang or a preventer to reduce the twist in the main and decrease rolling (Photo 2).

Most vangs are a four-part block-and-tackle. The vang attaches between the boom (15 to 20 percent of its length back from the mast) and a secure fitting on the mast just above the deck. A preventer is usually a

Photo 1 *Holding the jib out with a whisker pole is often the easiest, fastest, and safest way to sail downwind.*

three- or four-part block-and-tackle that attaches between the same area of the boom as a vang and a strong deck fitting on or near the gunwale, outboard of the mast. You can also use a strong line run from the boom to a block or fairlead on the rail and back to a cleat or winch in the cockpit. Make sure you can release the preventer quickly – a snap shackle on the boom works best – in case of an accidental gybe (Photo 3).

When sailing downwind it is best to pole out the jib to windward "wing-and-wing" style. Adjust the pole fore and aft to keep as much of the sail exposed to the wind as possible. Attach a topping lift or a spare halyard to the top of the pole and a single-part foreguy to the bottom of the pole to control pole height and keep it steady in rough conditions.

If you don't have a pole or don't wish to use one, you can still sail wing-and-wing. Pull the jib to the side of the boat opposite the main, trim it until the leech starts to curl toward the center of the boat, then ease it a little (Photo 4). If you overtrim the jib, it will collapse. Sailing this way without a whisker pole is tricky, but practicing is a good way to pass some time and expand your sailing knowledge.

If you are not sailing downwind, another option is to leave the jib behind the main, although it may become stalled and collapse. After trim-

Photo 2 *Without a boom vang or preventer to hold it down, the boom rises and twists the mainsail, decreasing the sail's efficiency.*

Photo 3 *A properly rigged preventer will hold the boom in place after an accidental gybe, giving the crew time to correct the situation.*

Photo 4 *Sailing wing-and-wing without a pole takes patience, but with a little practice it will speed your progress downwind.*

Photographs by Alyce M. Robinson

ming the main so the boom is perpendicular to the wind, try to trim the jib. Imagine there is a boom between the clew and the tack, and trim the jib until this "boom" is parallel to the main boom.

Steering.   In light to medium wind and flat water, steering downwind is quite simple. To help keep the boat tracking straight, line up the mast or forestay with an object in the distance. Practice keeping the boat pointed straight at your target, using as little rudder movement as possible. Eventually you'll develop a "feel" for when the boat is tracking straight. The boat's wake is another way to check your course; the straighter the wake, the better. Of course, a consistent compass course also indicates straight sailing.

When the wind pipes up, waves quickly get bigger and the boat requires more steering to stay on course. Keep in mind that in general the waves are going faster than the boat and tend to push the stern as they lift it. If the waves are coming from the starboard quarter, they will push the stern to port and the bow to starboard. As you feel a wave lift the stern, pull the helm to weather, center the helm when you are on top of the wave, and then push the helm to leeward as the back of the wave passes beneath you. The amount of pull and push depends on the conditions, and steering toward a landmark will help you stay on course.

Photo 5   *If your jib, when trimmed behind the main, tried to come across the boat, you are sailing by the lee and need to push the tiller toward the mainsail.*

Putting it together.   To sail directly downwind effectively and safely, you have to be aware of both sail trim and helmsmanship. Although this is the simplest point of sail in some respects, it can also be the most difficult. When you sail downwind, pay close attention to the sails, because even the smallest course change or wind shift can cause the sails to gybe and the boom to come swinging across the deck.

If you have trimmed the jib on the same side as the main and the jib tries to gybe itself, this is an indication that the boat is about to gybe (Photo 5). If this happens, you are sailing by the lee, and the boat may gybe on its own.

To solve the problem, simply push the tiller toward the main and head up. If you are sailing by the lee, another indication of an imminent gybe is a curl in the mainsail's leech. If the leech starts to curl toward the center of the boat, the sail is about to come across. Again, push the tiller toward the sail.

If your boat has a masthead fly, don't let it point toward the mainsail side of the boat when sailing downwind. If it does, you are sailing by the lee and the boat may gybe without your consent.

The easiest way to prevent an accidental gybe is to sail 20 to 25 degrees higher, or more toward the wind, than dead downwind. Depending on conditions, heading up may also decrease the rolling movement of your boat.

Sailing downwind safely takes extra concentration at first. But if you set up your boat properly with a preventer and practice steering a straight course, it can be a very pleasant and safe point of sail.

II

Race Tactics

Changing Gears to Maximize Boat Speed

Subtle changes in the set of a sail make all the difference

Derrick Fries

In one of my first collegiate regattas, I found myself competing in a 470 dinghy, a boat I knew little about. I was in awe of the many adjustments on a 470, and it was Bruce Nelson, who became a collegiate All-American sailor and is now a successful yacht designer, who taught me how to sail fast.

In the first race Bruce and his crew made a number of delicate moves to adjust the sails. When they saw a puff of wind ahead, they tightened the vang, trimmed in the jib and mainsheet, eased the traveler, and hiked out to stabilize the boat. Although I tried to do the same thing, my attempts were a disaster. I was not familiar with the systems on the boat, and I made the mistake of keeping my head down in the cockpit. I quickly lost my concentration and found myself sailing poorly. Unlike Nelson, I didn't know how to change the trim of the sail; I didn't know how to change gears.

On any body of water, the direction and velocity of the wind rarely remain steady for more than a few minutes at a time. This is particularly true in light air. Obviously, you cannot sail in light, shifty wind with the same sail settings you would use in a steady 15-knot breeze. More important, you need to have changed your trim - your gears - before a change in wind velocity reaches you.

When the wind speed changes, you must reshape the sail. On most boats this is done by first tightening the vang and the cunningham and then easing the traveler. But the real question is when to reshape the sail.

When to change gears. Here are two examples of skippers' reactions to puffs. Boat A is sailing upwind and suddenly finds itself in a puff. The skipper eases the main and jib to depower the boat while the crew hikes out hard to keep the boat level. Next the skipper trims the main and jib back in and asks the crew to tighten the vang and pull down on the cunningham. The skipper has *reacted* to the puff instead of anticipating it.

Now, take Boat B. This skipper is also sailing upwind. He or she sees a puff of wind ahead that is going to cross his path. Just before the puff hits, this skipper tightens the vang, pulls down on the cunningham, and eases out the traveler. He may even ease the main and jib slightly (although this depends on the boat type) to spill some air and keep the boat level. After the initial increase in velocity, he trims in the mainsheet and jibsheets, and the boat powers through the puff. In this case the skipper is acting *proactively*. If the two boats are very responsive dinghies, the distance Boat B can gain over Boat A by changing gears could be as much as three or four boat lengths.

Changing sail shape. Although every boat type is a little different, a good rule of thumb is to have the basic flat sail shape when the wind is 12 to 14 knots and water conditions are smooth. As the wind increases above that speed, you can ease both the outhaul and the cunningham to get a little more draft and power in the sail to go through waves. However, once the wind speed gets above 18 knots, in most boats you should again work toward a flatter sail shape.

Start with the middle range - 12 to 14 knots of wind and flat water - and work out the appropriate shapes on either side of that range. As the wind increases above 14 knots, make the sail a little fuller with a little more draft. Over 18 knots it should get flatter again. Between 7 and 12 knots a fuller shape works best. Below 7 knots you want to again flatten the sail a little bit (see figure).

Even though these changes in draft are relatively small, they can have a big effect on boat speed. The important concept is that the shape and draft of the sail should change as the wind changes. And at the greatest distance, above and below the middle 12- to 14-knot range, in almost all cases the sail should have a flatter shape.

Implementation. When you are sailing upwind in puffy conditions, estimating the strength of the puffs will help you decide what shaping elements are most important. On most boats the vang and the traveler have a great influence on shape, and sheeting in the jib and main once the puff has hit is also very important. You'll have to experiment to determine which are the most important sail shaping controls on your boat. Here's how to proceed when you see a puff coming:

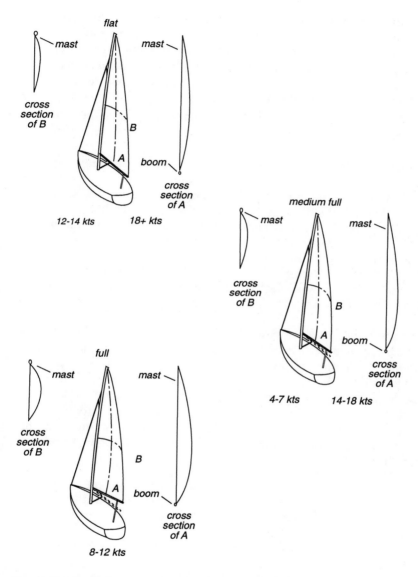

Fig. 1 *The shape of a mainsail is determined by the amount of wind and the water conditions. On most boats, in smooth water with winds of 12 to 14 knots, the mainsail should be set up with its basic designed shape (flat). When the wind goes above or below this range or sea conditions change, the sail shape should be altered to the general shapes shown here. The shapes shown are only approximate. Different boats and different sails will have differently designed shapes.*

- Move the mainsail traveler down and tighten the vang. Make these adjustments quickly, smoothly, and at the same time, to minimize disruption in the airflow over the sail.
- Do not make too many adjustments. In a two-person boat, use the vang and the traveler; in a one-person Laser, use the vang and perhaps the cunningham.
- As soon as you have sailed through the puff, reverse the process immediately by easing out the same lines.

Practice.   Once you set priorities for your trim adjustments, you need to practice them. Try to get yourself to the point where you are sailing on automatic pilot. When the wind speed is going to change, you should be ready and know immediately what to do. One good drill is to steer the boat blindfolded while you adjust the trim. Obviously, you must have a safety boat next to you if you are sailing your boat alone. If you have a crew, have them watch your adjustments.

During practice, work on the actual motions that you make to perform the task. If you are a singlehanded sailor, you might need to move forward in the boat to adjust the vang. Learn how to do that smoothly and gracefully, without jiggling the boat and interrupting airflow.

One of the drills I like best involves first establishing a benchmark time for a beat upwind to a mark. Then, assuming there is reasonably steady air, you make adjustments. If you sail the same beat 7 to 10 times, you will get a good feel for what changes reduce the time and improve your speed.

Since constantly changing wind speed is the norm, take a systematic approach to changing gears on your own boat. Break the process down into prediction and implementation, then go out and practice what you have learned. After a period of time, these concepts will become a natural part of your sailing repertoire.

Finding the Upwind Passing Lanes

Even with a bad start, you can get back in the race

Brad Dellenbaugh

───────────

It's great to dream about grabbing the front row at the start and never missing a shift until you cross the finish line. Reality is often far different, and at times you'll figure out how well you're doing by counting up from the rear of the fleet instead of down from the leader. When you find yourself in this situation, you need to decide how to pass boats on the weather leg and work you way back up through the fleet.

Remember that big gains (and losses) often come from the moves you make on the upwind legs. This means you should master the principles of upwind sailing.

Have a game plan.   Before the start, accumulate information about winds and currents across the race course. Use your observations to create a game plan for the first beat. If the right side of the course is favored, start so you can get to the right side. If the left side is favored, stay on starboard tack after the start to get to the left. Either way, you'll need to be positioned so you have clear air off the line.

Don't get caught up in the "which end of the line is favored" game and allow that uncertainty to dictate your start. Rather, focus on where you want to be *after* the start. If you get pinned and find yourself sailing away from the line to the wrong side of the course, you haven't planned enough.

If you don't know which side of the course is favored, stay near the middle. This gives you the flexibility to sail to whichever side seems to work better as you go up the beat.

Look for wind velocity.   Always sail to the area with the most wind. Once you are in higher velocity, play all the wind shifts. Two to three minutes before the start, stand up and look up the course to see where the water looks darker (which indicates more wind) and whether there are any significant puffs coming that you should get to right after the start. Don't chase any puff that will pass in front of you.

Prepare for a bad start.   If you find yourself with a second row start, have a bailout plan ready. First, see which boats are on your windward quarter. If you have to duck only the first row of boats, tack onto port right away. If you also have to duck under all the other boats that got bad starts, hold your tack until some of them clear out of the way.

The most important thing to remember here is to stay with your game plan. Always sail in lanes of clear wind that will let you stick with your plan. Unless there's a wind shift, the favored side of the course doesn't change just because you get a bad start.

Understand lateral separation.   Lateral separation is the sideways distance between you and another boat. The greater your lateral separation, or leverage, the greater your gain or loss if the wind shifts. The boat to windward gains if the wind shifts toward it, because the shift will leave it

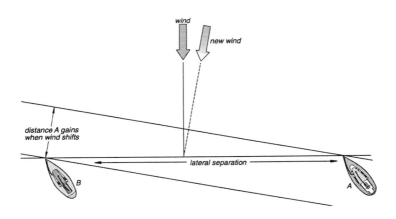

Fig. 1   *When two boats are even in a race, they are equally far upwind. If the wind shifts to the right, the inside boat (A) gains because it is now farther upwind. If the wind shifts to the left, boat B will gain upwind.*

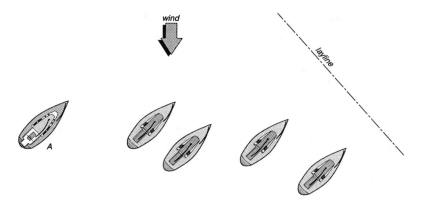

Fig. 2 *When you are sailing to a layline, position yourself on the windward quarter (A) to keep your options wide open.*

farther upwind. For example, the favored boat on a 10-degree wind shift gains 25 percent of the lateral separation between the two boats if the boat tacks through 90 degrees. If two boats are 20 boat-lengths apart and the wind shifts to the right 10 degrees, the boat on the inside of the shift will gain five boat lengths (Fig. 1). This is why boats get so spread out on a beat.

If you aren't sure what the wind is going to do, keep your lateral separation small. Although you give up maximum gain, you also reduce your risk. If you are sure you know what the wind will do, sail toward the expected shift and maximize lateral separation so you gain as much as possible when the shift comes.

Watch the layline.   Unless you are leading the race and covering your competition, it's rare that anything good comes from getting on a layline until you are actually approaching the mark. It is almost impossible to pick an accurate layline from a distance, and if you get lifted, you will have overstood the mark and wasted all that distance. If you get headed, you will lose ground on all boats that were sailing toward the shift.

You do want to get over to a layline eventually, and that's when you want to position yourself on the windward quarter of other boats going toward the layline. Because they will get to the layline first, they will have fewer options (Fig. 2).

Find the passing lane.   At times you will need to use aggressive tactics to pass a boat or boats on the windward leg. If you are not being covered tightly by the boat ahead, you have a number of options. If you are sure the side of the course to which you are sailing is the favored side, sail fast in that direction and maximize your lateral separation. If you are not sure about the wind, position yourself just to the inside of the boat ahead. If the wind shifts favorably, you will gain, and if it shifts unfavorably, you will minimize your loss. If the boat ahead is going in the direction you think is favored, keep your air clear and stay with it.

If the boat ahead is covering you tightly, there are several ways to get past it. The first is to foot through to leeward to clear air – if you don't have to reach off too much or for too long. If the boat is directly in front of you or on your lee bow, you can try sailing in the "pinch" mode for a short time to climb up to windward into a clear lane. If neither move works, try making two tacks. Always come out of the first tack with a lot of speed on, and if your competition tacks to cover you, tack back while the other boat is still trying to build speed after the first tack. If you do this properly, you can foot fast on port and get through to clear air when the other boat tacks again (Fig. 3).

If you are about to make a tack, never telegraph your moves to the other boat. If you see that the boat ahead is about to sail into a large set of waves, try to tack at that point. The other boat may delay its tack to rebuild speed. If it does tack, the boat will be very slow, and once you are up to speed you should tack back again.

Another good close-in move is to use a third boat as a blocker. Here you time your tack so that if the covering boat tacks to cover you, it ends up sailing into the bad air of the blocker boat, and this lets you escape (Fig. 4).

If you find yourself in the back of the fleet after the start, don't abandon your game plan and take a miracle flyer. Instead of trying to gain everything back at once, gradually work your way back up through the fleet using my comeback rules:

1. Think positively. If you make a mistake, don't focus on how you blew it. Concentrate on what's ahead of you and how you're going to catch up. Constantly think about how you will catch the next boat or group of boats right until you cross the finish line.

2. Never be greedy. If you're behind, try to get back a small amount on every leg. The biggest mistake you can make is to sail away from the fleet simply to maximize your leverage. Doing so overlooks the real strategic considerations that always get you around the course faster.

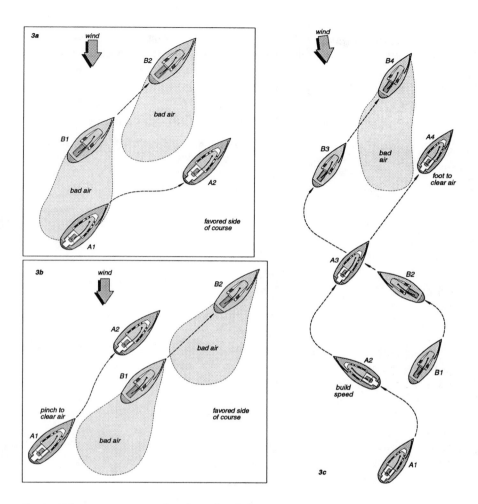

Fig. 3 *When you want to get by a boat ahead of you, you can either (a) foot to leeward, (b) pinch up to windward, or (c) make two tacks and come out of the first one with a lot of speed.*

3. Assess every risk. If you have a chance to pass 10 boats and risk losing only one, go for it. But if the risk outweighs the gain, be conservative. Cover the group behind you while you wait for a better opportunity. Always remember the big picture.

4. Keep looking for better wind velocity and favorable wind shifts. Use the boats around you to help spot wind coming down the course. If you can identify a pattern of wind shifts, play them to your advantage.

5. Go to the side of the course that can help you the most and hurt you the least. Work the wind or current on that side.

6. Avoid laylines. In the last two tacks to the windward mark of the finish line, if you keep your flexibility, you can pick up a lot of boats by playing the wind shifts. Never get caught in the parade of boats on a starboard tack layline.

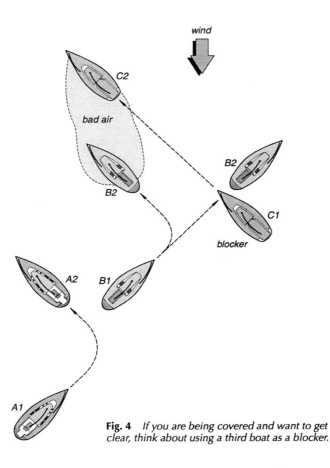

Fig. 4 *If you are being covered and want to get clear, think about using a third boat as a blocker.*

7. Sail in clean air, and plan one or two tacks ahead so you keep your lanes clear on those tacks.

8. Let other boats make mistakes and take risks; those are the boats you will pass. Try to close up the distance on boats ahead so you can attack them on the downwind leg.

9. Finally, believe that you are capable of passing all the boats that are ahead of you.

The next time you find yourself somewhere back in the fleet in the cheap seats, don't yell, pout, or whine. Get yourself and your crew psyched. Stick to the tactics and guidelines I've mentioned and start grinding down the competition ahead of you. That's how the top sailors do it.

How to Play the Downwind Angles

Instruments and courses play a crucial role off the wind

Jim Marshall

Racing downwind can be a very rewarding experience because you can get far bigger gains sailing off the wind than you can sailing upwind. But it can also be very frustrating. Sorting out the correct downwind approach takes all the tools available – accurate instrumentation, good polars, and your own senses – to monitor your progress and fine tune your performance.

The efficiency of your sails and rig sets limits on your close-hauled potential. But when you sail downwind in light air, there's a wide range of possible sailing angles, and often the correct angle is not obvious. You can sail farther off the wind to get closer to the mark, but this is often slower than sailing a higher course. Reaching up a bit adds distance to the mark but may also get you more boat speed. How do you find the best downwind sailing angle?

Sensory feedback. The sense of feel is always important at the helm, but it's especially so when you're steering downwind. For example, in six knots of true wind, the apparent wind speed for a 35-footer sailing upwind is about 10 knots, but downwind it's only about four knots. If true wind speed increases to eight knots while you're sailing upwind, apparent wind speed increases to 13 knots. But downwind the apparent wind speed increases only one knot. Your sensory perceptions are hard-pressed to recognize such subtle differences.

Other forms of feedback are diminished when sailing downwind. You may have some pressure on the helm going upwind, but there should be hardly any pressure sailing downwind. Upwind, the jibsheet and the mainsheet may be highly loaded, but sailing downwind in light-to-moderate conditions, the spinnaker and mainsail can usually be trimmed by hand. The strongest sensory feedback often comes through the spinnaker sheet, so it should be the spinnaker trimmer's responsibility to be aware of boat speed and sailing angle. Good coordination between the helmsman and the trimmer is critical and is often the difference between a fast boat and a slow one.

Instrument feedback.   When sensory feedback is decreased, accurate instrumentation becomes even more important. That's why you should carefully tune your instruments, especially the wind sensors, to make sure you get accurate information. After conducting a lot of tests on many different boats, I have found the best distance above the top of the mast for the sensors is six to seven percent of P (the mainsail luff length). This keeps the instruments out of the airflow that's been disturbed by the sailplan.

As with any tool, the quality of the wind sensor determines the effectiveness of the instrument. You must check the bearings that support the anemometer cups regularly. I was once sailing on San Francisco Bay and noticed my anemometer cups weren't responding the way they had earlier in the season. When I checked the bearings, I found they were full of dirt; dust in the air had accumulated in the bearings and had almost clogged them. Also check the windvane, because its shaft can accumulate grit, which in time will reduce its ability to indicate wind direction accurately.

Polar diagrams.   A polar diagram is a circular graph in which all measurements start at the origin, or center, of the graph. You find any point on a polar diagram by moving out from the origin in a specific direction, which is the true wind angle, and a specific distance from the center, which is boat speed. Each plotted curve is for a given true wind speed (Fig. 1).

This is another reason that you must have accurate information from your instruments: You must have a solid basis from which to apply your polar diagrams. Polars are generated by velocity prediction programs (VPP) and are widely used by naval architects in the design process. VPPs are also at the heart of the International Measurement System (IMS). You can get polars for your boat from most any naval architect, or the company that designed the boat, or through yachting organizations that specialize in maintaining data on your boat's design and class. A check with a local yacht club can also help.

The downwind sailing angles for most displacement boats change dramatically as true wind speed changes from nine to 14 knots. Up to about

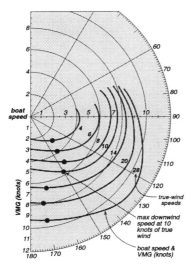

Fig. 1 *A polar diagram graphically shows the speed and angle a boat should achieve when sailing downwind. For example, when sailing at a true-wind angle of 150 degrees in 10 knots of wind, the target speed for this boat is about 5.8 knots.*

nine knots, most polars show the true wind angle for optimum downwind performance is about 145 degrees. However, between nine and 14 knots, this angle changes dramatically, increasing from 145 degrees to about 168 degrees. This change in the sailing angle is called the "downwind cliff." It begins at different wind speeds depending on displacement; for an ultralight-displacement boat (ULDB), the cliff starts at a higher wind speed than it does for a heavy-displacement boat. However, a good rule of thumb is that the cliff begins at about 10 knots for most boats (Fig. 2). For each additional knot of true-wind speed on the downwind cliff, you can sail about five degrees lower.

You can tell whether your instruments are in sync with the boat's polars by testing your downwind sailing angles in a known wind speed. Start by sailing a course on which your spinnaker is drawing nicely and note the speed. Now head off a few degrees, retrim the sails, and watch your boat speed; it should drop a bit. Head off some more, retrim, and record the speed. Keep repeating this exercise until boat speed suddenly drops dramatically. The spinnaker will probably no longer fly well, and the boat will begin to wallow.

This angle is the point at which the sailplan loses a high percentage of its drive. You should not sail below this true wind angle at the particular wind speed. For most boats the optimum true wind sailing angle for that wind speed is about five to 10 degrees higher than the drop-off angle.

After you have conducted this exercise over a wide range of wind strengths, you will see how closely the predicted optimum downwind sailing angles on the polars match up with the actual angles. If the polars don't match the actual angles, chances are the instruments are reading inaccurately. If they do match up pretty well, you can have confidence in them and use the predicted angles aggressively on the race course.

Polars also provide your downwind target boat speeds. Since the optimum true wind angle remains fairly constant at about 145 degrees up to nine knots of true wind speed, knowing what speed you should achieve is vital. Look at Figure 2 and note the large change in predicted boat speed for each knot of true wind speed increase. In this case, for every knot increase in true wind speed, you should gain 0.6 knot of boat speed. Target boat speeds provide both helmsman and crew with immediate performance goals.

Target boat speeds focus the effort of the crew on efficiently shifting gears, accelerating the boat, and getting to the target speed. They also help decelerate the boat efficiently when the wind drops.

Accurate polars and target speeds can make the difference between knowing you will go faster in a puff and knowing precisely how much faster you can go in that puff. This knowledge can produce big gains anytime you sail downwind on a race course.

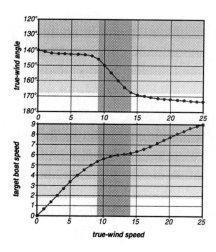

Fig. 2 *The plot of target boat speed against true-wind angle and speed for a typical 35-footer (top graph) shows the three major levels of boat speed relative to wind speed at 0 to 9 knots, 9 to 14 knots, and 14 knots and above. Note how the "downwind cliff," the increasing sailing angle needed to maintain target boat speed as true-wind speed increases, begins at 9 knots and tapers off at 14 knots.*

Accelerated Roll-Tacking

This neat trick gives you better performance

Michael Tamulaites

⬛

Round-bottomed racers like the Laser, Finn, Thistle, Tech Dinghy, 470, and a myriad of others were designed to be tacked very easily. What many of the designers didn't know, however, was that in the 1970s a group of overachieving young sailors would take it upon themselves to introduce roll-tacking and make these boats jump a level in tacking efficiency.

A roll tack uses the boat, its sails, and its appendages to best advantage through a tack. Roll-tacking also minimizes the amount of force you have to use on the rudder to turn the boat. In light air it is not uncommon for a boat to come out of a well-executed roll tack faster than it went into it. Tacking fast on any boat is a key to racing success, so much so that even the crew of the mighty 120-foot America's Cup racer *New Zealand* gave roll-tacking a shot.

The speed advantage of roll-tacking over just pushing the helm down and switching sides is considerable, but when tactical considerations are brought into the equation, roll-tacking becomes a lethal weapon. Imagine heading for the starboard layline on port tack into a wall of starboard-tackers and throwing a lee-bow roll tack on some unsuspecting soul, leaving him or her in your bad air. Not roll-tacking and losing five or six boats by ducking to find a hole to tack into is a poor alternative.

Roll tacks can be used effectively on the starting line as well. For example, if you are on port tack approaching a line of starboard-tackers heading for the starting line, you can, with a well-timed roll tack, tack to leeward, maintain your speed, and keep your air clear as the gun is fired.

The reasons for roll-tacking are clear; the method is fairly straightforward. Although roll-tacking is effective in all wind conditions, it is most effective in light air. In general, when sailing upwind in light air – say, four to six knots – you should keep the boat slightly heeled to leeward, reducing wetted surface and helping the sail or sails fall into place. This sailing position sets you up well for a roll tack. To begin the tack, use your body weight to heel the boat even farther to leeward while using the tiller extension to help the tiller fall to leeward. As the mainsail begins to luff, start moving back to windward, leaving the tiller pushed to leeward. When the boom crosses the boat, hike out hard, preferably hard enough to get the seat of your pants wet.

As the sail begins to set on the new tack, ease the mainsheet enough to let you get under the boom and climb up to the new high side while facing forward. As you straighten the tiller, hike out hard to flatten the boat. As soon as the mast is vertical, lean in toward the center of the boat to regain leeward heel for fast light-air sailing (see photos).

A roll tack is faster than a conventional tack because it keeps the sails, rudder, and centerboard in almost constant motion. As you heel the boat hard to weather, the sail is operating at a higher angle of attack, creating additional forward force. Similarly, the centerboard's and, to a lesser extent, the rudder's motion through the water creates more forward force, especially if they have airfoil sections. Climbing up to the high side and hiking the boat down flat reverses the direction of this movement but creates even more force, which accelerates the boat out of the tack.

To practice roll-tacking, head out on the water during a light-to-medium-air day – say, six to eight knots of wind. Sail the boat upwind as you normally would in these conditions. Then, without easing the mainsheet, lean as far as you can toward the leeward side. As soon as the leeward rail touches the water, or when you feel the boat start to slow down, hike out hard to weather. The boat will accelerate dramatically. As it decelerates, start again by leaning toward the leeward side of the boat.

This maneuver will show you the effect of pulling the sail through the air and pushing the centerboard and rudder through the water. It will also show you how far and how long you should heel the boat to leeward before tacking. Remember that leaning in and hiking out fast without tacking, a false roll tack, is illegal in racing. Now you know why.

After a couple of false tacks, do a real one. Keep your body movement as smooth as possible. Lean in to help the boat head into the wind and push the tiller to leeward. When the boat slows slightly, hike out hard to windward without easing the mainsheet or moving the tiller. As the boat slows again after the tack, climb to weather quickly, ease the mainsheet

Before the tack, lean
in and heel the boat
and slowly start turn-
ing into the wind

As the boat comes
into the wind, lean
out hard to wind-
ward to get the rig
moving to windward

When the boat is on
the new tack,
release the sheet
and climb up to the
new windward side

Finally, hike to
windward to bring
the mast back to
vertical; then trim
for best speed

a few inches, and hike out to flatten the boat. After the boat accelerates, lean in to return to a fast light-air heel angle.

One of the best drills for improving your timing and speed across the boat during a tack, especially in small beach-type boats, is to head out on the water when it is glass flat, with little or no breeze. Heel the boat hard to leeward and complete a roll tack. But after hiking the boat flat on the new tack, stay hiked and go right into another tack. Keep repeating these tacks as long as you can or until your rhythm is disrupted, whichever comes first.

After taking a few gulps of water, try to analyze what made you stop. If it was boredom, you're well on your way to becoming a roll-tacker extraordinaire. If it was something else, go for a quick swim and start again.

Roll-tacking is a demanding but very rewarding maneuver. With practice you will be able to roll-tack without thinking about it, and you will be able to use your experience to put your boat in places on the race course you didn't think it would go.

Roll-Gybing for Speed

Another neat trick works from a different angle

Michael Tamulaites

Racing-dinghy sailors were the first to realize the advantages of roll-gybing. After mastering the roll tack for upwind performance, they discovered that rolling a boat during a gybe allowed them to maintain as much speed as possible through the maneuver and then to accelerate quickly to pre-gybe speed. This speed advantage, plus better control when the boom crosses the boat, makes roll-gybing a sensible maneuver for any sailor.

In a "traditional" gybe, many sailors simply pull the tiller away from the mainsail and wait for the boom to fly across the boat while everyone ducks and switches sides. The boat remains relatively flat through the maneuver and loses speed while the main crosses the boat and the rudder turns the boat, which creates rudder drag. With this type of gybe, you never know exactly when the boom will cross, and a significant amount of time elapses before the boat accelerates up to speed. Roll-gybing eliminates this speed loss and uncertainty.

The best way to learn how to roll-gybe is to sail on a broad reach in about six to eight knots of wind and flat water. Begin with the sail trimmed properly, on the verge of luffing, the boat relatively flat (no heel), and, if you have one, the centerboard at least halfway down (see photos). To start the gybe lean away from the mainsail so the boat starts to heel, or roll, to windward. The boat will naturally turn farther away from the wind, allowing you to turn the rudder without creating drag.

As the boat goes past a direct-downwind heading and begins to slowly head up toward the wind, forcefully trim the mainsheet. Pull it in enough

Photo 1

Photo 2

Photo 3

Begin the roll gybe by heeling the boat to windward and turning away from the wind (1). As the sail crosses the boat, move to the new windward side (2). As you cross the boat, switch the tiller and mainsheet in your hands. Then, after hiking the boat flat, trim the sail for speed (3).

to allow the wind to hit the back side of the mainsail and push the boom across the boat. Simultaneously, while facing forward, cross the boat and switch the tiller and mainsheet each to the opposite hand. When you are on the new windward side, hike out hard to flatten the boat quickly. The rudder will naturally want to straighten, which will keep rudder drag to a minimum.

Hiking out after the sail has gybed helps the boat accelerate to get back up to the speed it had before the gybe. Flattening the boat pulls the full sail to weather, making it act like a handheld fan to produce forward thrust. The appendages moving laterally through the water create a forward thrust of their own, and with the sail and appendages working together, the boat squirts forward like a watermelon seed.

When roll-gybing a small beach boat or two-person dinghy, the goal is to heel the boat to windward enough to get the windward rail, and therefore the seat of your pants, a bit wet before you start your move across the boat. With the boat heeled to windward so the rail is in the water, the sails and appendages are set up like a coiled spring for maximum propulsion. By jerking the mainsheet in quickly instead of waiting for the wind to push the boom across the boat, you can accurately control when the boat gybes, which makes for a safer maneuver.

Perfect timing is the key to roll-gybing, and practice is the only way to get your timing right. Keep the mainsheet trimmed at about a 45-degree angle to the boat's centerline, and try to go directly from one roll gybe into the next. You'll find that it's a tiring exercise, but you will also quickly feel how rolling the boat speeds the maneuver.

Roll-gybing a boat requires a fluid motion. With practice it will become second nature, and that will allow you to concentrate on either your competition or the scenery around you.

Get the Right Shapes for Heavy Air

Speed comes from more than just more wind

Ed Baird

―――――――――

When I sail in heavy air, I think about my boat speed only *after* I have a strong positive attitude and good boat handling. There's a reason for this. If you have a good attitude about going out in the rough stuff *and* you're good at boat handling, you'll more than likely wind up going pretty fast.

But first you need to have a solid understanding of the mechanics needed to get your boat going fast in the heavy stuff. Fortunately, there are some rules for getting good boat speed in these conditions.

Bearing off.   First, when going upwind, any boat is apt to have difficulty going forward and pointing well. The boat feels as if it's never in the groove; waves slow the boat down, and puffs keep knocking it over. The end result is that the boat tends to slide sideways.

When a boat starts pointing poorly in heavy air, the traditional reaction is to pull the sails in tighter. However, the reason the boat is pointing poorly is usually that the keel or centerboard has too much side force for the amount of water flowing past it. The foil gets stalled, or overloaded, by the large side forces being generated by the sails.

There are two ways to relieve the pressure on the keel or board and thereby reduce stalling. The first is to increase the speed of the water flowing over the foil, and the second is to reduce the side force. Bearing off is the way to accomplish both goals.

However, when you do bear off – and I'm talking about a course change of only one or two degrees – it is even easier for the wind to knock the boat down. To avoid this, you must adjust the sails.

The best way to trim the sails so they can help the boat go forward faster is to move them outboard. On a large racing boat, that means going to an outboard track for the jib and dropping the main traveler down. This will keep the sails at the same angle to the wind from bottom to top and will also relieve some of the pressure on the underwater foil. Now the sail forces will be moving the boat forward more and sideways less. In smooth water this is a fast way to go; it can also work in rough conditions, as long as the wind is relatively constant.

Twistings.   The big challenge comes when it's blowing and also puffy. When you think everything's okay, a big puff hits, and you run out of traveler and broach, or at least slow the boat. The whole sail luffs, then fills, then you broach and the sail luffs again.

In these conditions, the answer lies in sail twist. Whenever you twist a sail by easing the sheet, the leech of the sail opens up. Because it opens first at the top, twist has a direct effect on heeling. The more twist in the sail, the less heeling force.

When you are steering around large waves in puffy conditions, having some twist allows the boat to go through a broader range of headings with less change in heel. After you go over the top of a wave and bear off, the sail's power will increase only slightly if it is twisted. Then as you head up again, only a little power will go into heeling the boat; much more goes into driving it forward.

With a tighter leech, like the one you want to have in medium-air conditions, the sail will be either right or wrong. It will luff at the same time from top to bottom, and it will stall at the same time, too. But if you have a tight leech in blustery weather, the sails will luff every time you need to head up to go over a wave. The boat's power will be reduced, which will stand the boat straight up. Then as you head off down the top of the wave to get going again, the sails will fill all at once. That will heel you over, which forces the boat sideways.

But once you put a little twist in the sail up high, the boat will settle down and make much better progress. The trick, of course, is to put in just the right amount of twist. Because it is impossible to talk in specifics, I'll give you an idea of how the boat should feel and react when things are set up right. If the boat has very little weather helm but must be steered a lot with rudder, you have too much twist in the mainsail. Too much twist will also make the boat seem as though it is standing up particularly straight and doesn't want to point well. While you will probably go fast, you will be sailing low.

If the leech is too tight, with inadequate twist, the boat will heel too much and will have lots of weather helm. Then, as the helm goes light, the sails will luff, and the boat will stand up. The range between luffing and excessive heeling will be very narrow. Both boat speed and pointing will suffer as you search for the "groove."

The bow will tend to jump off the top of a wave and then crash back down, which drops the speed even more. While you may be sailing high, you are not getting anywhere. Even worse, the boat feels very powerful while you feel very helpless.

When the sail has the correct amount of twist, the boat will feel lively but also controllable. It will go forward and have a comfortable helm, similar to what you usually have in moderate conditions. Getting hit by a puff and steering around waves won't knock the boat down. And instead of jumping off waves, the bow will want to follow the wave down its backside and won't heel excessively as it goes. Once the correct amount of twist is set, you can adjust the main with the traveler to help the boat point up, or to foot off if necessary.

As with all trimming, nothing should ever remain static. If the breeze builds or drops for over a minute or so, adjustments must be made. Usually it is the mainsheet that should be moved the most. But don't neglect the jib in larger wind-speed changes.

Reaching. Twisting all the sails more than you normally would allows the boat to move forward faster and heel less and reduces the effects of waves and puffs. This is particularly true if you are flying a spinnaker. You can put twist in the chute by keeping the tack, or pole, lower than the clew and by moving the sheet lead aft.

One technique that works well for jib-reaching in puffy conditions is to trim the jib with the spinnaker sheet and use the jibsheet as a tweaker. In the light spots, you can pull on the tweaker (jibsheet) to reduce twist until the power is right. When a puff hits, ease the main first, but once it's luffing, ease the jibsheet tweaker. The sail will twist quickly, which will keep boat speed high but control heel. This technique will require far less winch grinding after the puff has passed, and that can take seconds off your finish time.

When you are broad reaching and running in high winds, twist in the sails can become your enemy. Too much twist in the mainsail on a downwind leg can produce a force that can get the boat into a death roll. Keeping a tight leech prevents this. However, if a big puff or a wave starts to put you into a broach, having a tight leech will accelerate the process. This is why you should have someone standing by to release the vang and put twist in the main, which will keep the boat on its feet.

Much of your success sailing in high wind will come from practicing in those conditions. Knowing when to head up to take a wave and when to head off after it has passed comes only from practice. But once you have confidence in your boat handling and in your ability to control the shape of your sails in these conditions, you will be on your way to achieving some great finishes when the breeze starts to build.

Sailing the Shifting Northwesterly

The wind that often drives you crazy can be tamed

Mike Huck, Jr.

The unstable air that always follows a cold front gives sailors a chance to prove their ability to handle major wind shifts. As a cold front moves through, the fast-moving cold air that makes up the front rams into the warmer air in front of it. This pile-up causes eddies that eventually appear on the water surface as sudden lifts and headers.

If the cold front is strong, the strong northwesterly wind in North America that accompanies it can also present control problems. But your main focus must be on figuring out where the wind will come from next. This provides a tremendous opportunity for crews who know how to handle changing wind velocity and direction.

Upwind. Anticipation is your key to success sailing upwind in shifty air. Although there usually is no set pattern for the eddies that drop down to create the gusts on the water, it is not hard to see the gusts coming at you on the surface of the water (Fig. 1). You have to be able to spot gusts early, and the crew must be ready to take action well before the wind arrives. When a puff hits, you want to have the sails eased for the increased wind and have the crew already up on the rail and hiking out hard.

As your boat's speed increases in a gust, you should tighten the sheet and the vang and take in on the cunningham. These three sail controls can help you move to top speed more quickly.

Header or lift? The eddies and gusts from a northwesterly are fairly compact, and it is easy to see their relative direction as they move over the water surface. Any gust that approaches you from directly ahead is likely to be a header, as is one that has passed by just in front of you. Both the leading and trailing edges of a gust cell change direction as they spread out over the water.

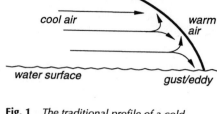

Fig. 1   *The traditional profile of a cold front pushing in behind a warm front shows how cool air pushes down to the water surface and creates shifting eddies and gusts.*

You can avoid these headers either by tacking as soon as you feel the effects of the gust or by setting your boat up to point as high as possible and simply steering above the gust. Getting this "extra height," or pointing ability, from your boat may be enough to get you above the edge of the gust even as the boats below you are being pushed down onto a lower course as the gust spreads out on top of them.

If you don't have the luxury of heading up to get above a potential header that's coming your way – if, for example, you are to leeward and outside a group of boats, and you see a gust that is definitely going to be a header – do the opposite from lifting up and sailing around it. Power up the sails, head off a little, and try to move ahead of the boats above you.

Your goal is to reach the leading edge of what is going to be a header before your competitors. This gives you the chance to get some extra life out of the wind on the other tack before your fellow racers reach the new shift.

You can spot a lift by watching how it moves toward you across the water. A puff that is heading toward the side of your boat is likely to be a lift (Fig. 2). If you can see this developing a good distance away, you can get the crew and the boat ready to go into the acceleration mode. First ease the sheets and squeeze up to the gust; then trim in and fall off to your normal close-hauled course as the boat begins to pick up speed. Your next challenge will be to spot the next wind shift and capitalize on it – even while your crew is hooting and hollering with your success on the first one.

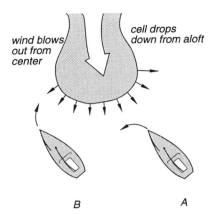

Fig. 2 *When a gust comes down and hits the water surface, it spreads out; the wind direction depends on where you are relative to the gust. In this case the gust is approaching boat A from the front, and boat A will be headed. But it is also hitting boat B from the side, producing a nice lift.*

Off the wind (reaching). Playing the gusts properly off the wind allows you to either build up some more distance or make up for an error you committed earlier. There are only a few great opportunities for a good clean pass on a reach, so it doesn't make sense to jump out to windward of someone just as a big header rolls on top of you. The header will pull the apparent wind forward, and you will have to sail that much farther ahead of your opponent before you can blanket him with your sails.

However, if you see a lift coming at you from the windward side, you should plan to go for it. You do this by "slingshotting" in front of your competitor like a race car driver on an oval track. Make your move just before the puff hits. Your wind shadow will move forward when the wind moves aft and hit the boat below. This makes it easier for you to shoot by before the other boat gets enough wind to accelerate to match your speed (Fig. 3).

If you don't get clear ahead of the other boat, don't worry. As the wind swings back, it tends to keep your wind shadow aimed at the boat to leeward.

Downwind. Your opportunities to use a gust to your advantage while running are not as great as they are on other points of sail. Your job here is to make sure your boat is in front of a gust when it comes down the course. If you see one coming on the other side of the course, try to work over to it and catch it before the other boats do. Big gains are made when you can spot a gust and get over to it early.

Watching for and playing the puffs in a northwesterly is a skill developed by practicing in those conditions. You may not always hit the gusts and shifts right, but even if you hit them correctly 75 percent of the time, you'll be in great shape. Remember that the seemingly random nature of the wind's speed and direction after a frontal passage can actually make racing in it easier for you.

Rapid wind shifts confuse crews who don't know what to look for and can't react when they do get a shift. But they can be your ticket to a big lead at the finish.

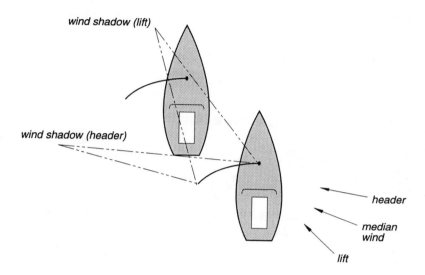

Fig. 3 *When you are sailing on a reach in a shifting wind, you don't want to try to pass on a header. Wait for a lift, because as the wind moves aft, your wind shadow moves forward and blankets the other boat. Before your opponent can accelerate, you can blanket him and "slingshot" ahead.*

Sailing Drills to Make You Faster

For best results, practice, practice; then for a change, practice again

Todd Berman

━━━━━━━━━━

All of us sail and race because we enjoy the satisfaction of being on the water with our friends and crews. When you get into a racing situation, however, particularly in either a Performance Handicap Racing Fleet or a local club event, it is interesting to see how few crews have done much practice on the water.

In any racing situation there are three areas in which it is essential to have good crew work and understanding among the players. The three areas are (1) knowledge about the boat's equipment, (2) good teamwork (and team bonding), and (3) good sail trim and boathandling.

You build these skills by working at them. In the area of building teamwork, the first thing to do is to make the crew feel as though they are really part of a team. Define realistic goals for the boat for the season and make sure everyone knows that it is the team that is going to achieve these goals. Always credit the entire crew when any of these goals are achieved.

You can do some of this goal setting and team development early in the season by having what might be called a "psych-up" session. Have the crew over for an evening, get everyone comfortable, then brief the crew on your season's plans, schedules, and goals. You can hand out crew shirts at this time and allocate specific responsibilities.

Have the sail trimmers be in charge of making sure sails are repaired if there is something wrong. Have the tactician be responsible for all charts and instruments. The bowman can be in charge of making sure the running rigging is sound and works well. Obviously, the job doesn't have to match the position, but what is important is distributing the responsibility among everyone so that each member is involved.

The second way to build crew confidence and teamwork is to schedule a work day on the boat. Get the crew – all of them – working on a specific project; the bottom is a good one. It's important that everyone be involved, because the benefits of speed that come from this effort are everyone's responsibility, not that of just a few who are normally charged with the maintenance on the boat.

Later in the work sessions, have the mast man and pit man mark the positions of all the key control lines and the best height for the inboard end of the spinnaker pole and the pole lift. Check all the rigging for signs of wear, and take everything off the boat and put back only what you think is necessary or required. Then give the boat a thorough scrub inside and out. This sounds like a lot of work, and in some ways it is. But it is the kind of work that helps build crew teamwork and gets everyone involved in preparing the boat for racing.

Finally, if you really want to carry through with your program, you have to get out and practice your sailhandling on the water, where all the action takes place. One of the best ways to improve your overall ability in this training phase is to have a "coach" come out with you as you go through your practice sessions. A coach need not be a professional, but he or she should be a knowledgeable observer who can make tactful and constructive observations. If possible, have the individual stand out of the way – near the backstay is a popular spot – and look for any inefficient motion, taking notes on ways to improve teamwork and speed in the sailhandling and trim areas.

Out on the water, three basic drills can improve your crew's sailhandling skills. The first is the *snaking drill*, which is nothing more than having a particular sail combination up and the helmsman slowly changing course at random, while crew members trim the sails at the correct angle.

It is very important in this drill that everyone take the helm for a period of time. For example, have the spinnaker trimmer steer while the helmsman trims the chute. This should give each crew member a better feeling for the jobs the others are performing.

Make sure none of the course changes is abrupt or complicated. Your only goal here is to have everybody feel the motion of the boat as the helmsman alters course and respond by trimming in or easing out smoothly. The helmsman should start out by making the turning motions slowly, then gradually build up speed as the crew's coordination and trimming skills improve. But never make any maneuver faster than it would be in an actual racing situation.

The second drill, which I call the *sailhandling drill*, is a little more complicated. For this exercise you need to set two marks in the water. Position them on a perfect windward-leeward axis far enough apart so that it takes you about 15 minutes to sail from the leeward mark back to the windward mark. You should use this drill to practice tacking, sail changes, and spinnaker work. Here again you should start very slowly when turning the boat and speed up the movements only when everyone aboard is comfortable with that speed.

The final drill is the *starting drill*. For this one you need only one mark. In this drill you can practice starting from a dead stop and accelerating to full speed. Begin a three-minute countdown and try to arrive at the mark going at full speed at the end of the three minutes. This drill helps you perfect your timing and acceleration skills, and it also teaches the crew to be both flexible and fast in their trimming.

Try several different approaches to the line. Luffing on starboard tack, then speeding up and going for the line is one good variation. Another is to assume you are going to arrive at the line early, with less than one minute to go. How do you slow the boat down, and how do you get that information to the crew? How you accelerate in the last 30 seconds is an important variation. Coming in on port tack, then tacking onto starboard with 1.5 minutes left is another good practice move. Your objective is to vary your approach speed but still hit the line at the moment the gun goes off, moving at full speed.

Each of these on-the-water drills should be practiced for a period of time. For example, if you have a day to practice, you could take an hour for the snaking drill, about three hours for the sailhandling drill, and then spend another hour on starts.

The reason for these drills should be clear. They are the basis for every sailing maneuver you will do on the race course, and the only way to get everyone familiar with what might happen is to go out on the water and make things happen in a practice session.

So if you want to do more than just wish you could do well this summer, make time now to get out and go through these basic on-the-water sailing-trim exercises. When you do get up against the rest of the fleet in competition, your crew will have the confidence and knowledge they need to get up on the starting line in good shape. Then you can steer and trim your way around the course in winning form.

Ease, Hike and Trim for Gusts

Handling the gusts and lulls will maximize your speed

Ed Baird

A naval architect once told me that on a well-designed 40-footer, for every 1,000 pounds of force generated by the sails, only 17 are actually pulling the boat forward. The rest of the force is spent heeling the boat and pushing it sideways.

While there may be genuine argument about this number, the point is that very little of the sail's force is working for the boat upwind. Most of the sail's forces are hurting it. Once you know how sails work, you can appreciate why they should rarely be in a static position. They should always be moving, responding to changes in the wind speed. The best time to really see these effects is when you get either a gust or a lull.

A sail is most effective when the wind is blowing across it on both the windward and leeward sides. If the sail is poorly trimmed to the wind, either it luffs, which generates virtually no power, or it stalls. In this case the sail still moves the boat, but the boat moves at a much slower pace than its potential.

A sail's curve basically determines its ability to develop horsepower. The greater the curve, the more powerful it is. But the flatter the sail, the closer it can be trimmed to the wind. As sailors, we are always trying to balance these two variables, moving the boat using as much power (fuller shape) as we can, but minimizing the drag as much as possible by using a flatter shape.

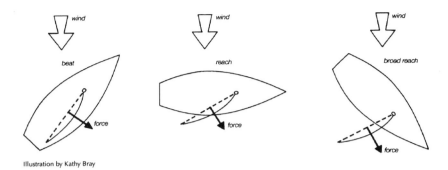

Illustration by Kathy Bray

Fig. 1 *You can make a rough determination of the driving force of a mainsail by drawing an imaginary line from the luff to the leech of the sail and then running a perpendicular to leeward. This is the direction in which the sail is going to pull the boat, without the influence of the keel or centerboard.*

But we racers already know that. Let's get to the hard part: Where is the power moving us? Imagine you're looking down on a mainsail. Draw an imaginary line from the luff to the leech, and then draw a perpendicular to leeward off that line. That line represents the angle toward which the sail is directing most of its power. Trim that sail at various angles to the wind, and you can see how the "force" line moves around (Fig. 1).

In the broad-reaching mode, you see the sail's force line is taking you exactly where you want to go – downwind. When reaching, even though the sail is helping you, it's also obvious you need a keel or centerboard to keep from sliding sideways.

The upwind configuration describes the conditions that the naval architect was talking about. The sail force is directed almost exactly sideways to where the boat is trying to go. Good sail trim and good underwater foils – keel and rudder – are critical to boat speed on this heading.

Once you understand the "force" concept, you also know that any time you can ease the sail out a little, still head the way you want to go, and not luff the sail, you get there faster.

When a gust hits.   Now let's change the picture slightly and show what happens when you get an increase in wind speed from a gust. When a puff or gust hits, several things happen. First, the increased wind speed gives the sail on the boat more power. When that happens, the boat heels more and tries to head up. To correct for this, you use more rudder, which, in turn, adds more drag. All this takes place in more wind, which should mean that you are accelerating. If you are alert, you can eliminate these bad effects and add to your speed at the same time. First, though, look more closely at that puff.

When you get increased wind, the sails feel what is called an apparent lift, which means the apparent wind comes aft and you can head up higher. Once your boat speed catches up with the new wind speed, of course, things generally go back to the same angles as before. But with the initial shot provided by a puff or gust, the apparent lift can stall the sail and add a lot to the sideways force it generates (Fig. 2).

Now you can see how the words "ease," "hike," and "trim" fit together. When you first get a puff, the boat has more power and the sail is stalled. This creates a heeling force and sideways movement. That is why quickly easing the sail when the puff hits solves both problems. When the sail is eased, its directional force line rotates forward. That, as we now know, is what helps drive the boat faster and reduces the amount it heels.

As the boat starts to move more quickly, the sail begins to feel a slight header as the apparent wind begins to move forward again; that is when you run the sail back in to its previous state of good trim.

In between these two moves, however, a good small boat sailor hikes out to counteract the increased heel. On bigger boats or if you're already hiked out, you can simply let the sail out a little farther. If you do this

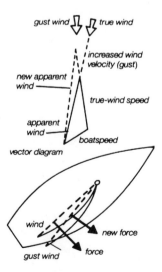

Illustration by Kathy Bray

Fig. 2 *When a gust hits your boat, it takes time for boat speed to climb. This is why the apparent wind moves aft in an apparent lift, as the vector diagram shows. So easing the main slightly not only keeps the main from stalling and the boat from heeling, but also moves the "force line" in a more forward direction.*

maneuver properly, the boat stays at virtually the same angle of heel, and the keel or centerboard can work at maximum efficiency. Smooth crew work above the water means the boat's hull and foils move easily through the water.

The smaller or lighter the boat, the more aggressively you trim the sails. A good Laser sailor, for instance, might appear to be very awkward, what with all the jerking and trimming going on. But if the sailor is good, the mast angle of the boat will barely change as the wind increases and decreases.

On larger ocean racers, speed builds more slowly, but you follow the same trim procedures. On bigger boats you usually use the traveler to ease the main, while on smaller boats you use the mainsheet. When you are sailing on the wind, you use only the main to depower. The jib should be trimmed in, but the clew should be positioned as far outboard as possible to help pull the boat forward.

"Ease, hike, and trim" is a lesson not just for collegiate dinghy sailors, but for everyone. Try it on your boat, and you'll see your speed climb whenever the wind picks up.

How to Depower Your Rig

Less can be more on a racing boat

Steve Benjamin

Knowing how to depower your rig when the wind increases above a certain velocity is an important element in your sailing repertoire. You can actually increase your boat's speed by depowering.

There are two basic ways to reduce the power of the sails. The first is to reduce the amount of sail area exposed to the wind by reefing the mainsail or reducing the size of the headsail by rolling it up or changing down to a smaller size jib. The second is by making one or more of six possible adjustments to the sails and rig. Let's look at these options.

Reduce sail depth.   Flattening the sails is one of the most effective ways to depower. A quick adjustment is to increase mast bend, which dramatically flattens the mainsail; the distance between the luff and the leech is reduced as the mast bends backward. On most offshore racing boats the key controls for mast bend are the checkstays, the running backstay, and the permanent backstay (Fig. 1).

Two adjustments that flatten the bottom of the sails and reduce their power are tightening the outhaul on the main and moving the jib lead aft. Moving the lead aft also produces more twist. If the mainsail is vang sheeted, changing outhaul tension will not have a large effect on the sail's upper leech twist.

On fractionally rigged boats such as One-Tonners or Three-Quarter-Tonners, checkstays control the lower part of the mast, running backstays set the headstay tension, and the permanent backstay controls the upper mast bend. This system gives good control of the upper and lower sections of the spar and isolates the important variables of headstay tension.

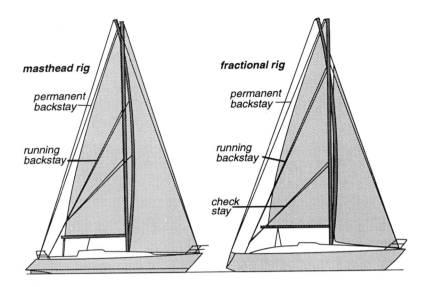

Fig. 1 *With a masthead rig, the permanent backstay controls the amount of headstay sag, and the running backstay and checkstays control the amount of mast bend. A fractional rig differs in that running backstays control headstay sag and the permanent backstay controls mast bend.*

Masthead-rigged boats also use checkstays to control lower mast bend; the runners, rather than the permanent backstay, are the primary control for upper mast bend. The permanent backstay is used to tension the headstay and control headstay sag. While tensioning the backstay can increase mast bend considerably, this tendency can be counteracted with increased runner tension.

Using a vang is also a good way to induce lower mast bend. As vang tension is increased, the boom is pulled forward and down. Downward pull at the gooseneck is opposed by the mast, but forward pull is transferred into bending movement.

Vang tension is as effective on offshore racing boats as it is in dinghies. As long as the vang is eased before bearing away and tension is applied within safe limits, there is no reason why using a vang should be unsafe on offshore boats.

One key element in using mast bend to flatten the sail is that the sail must fit the spar. If it does not, it will become distorted at one or more places as mast bend is increased. Try to correct distortions with rig tuning, or consult your sailmaker. Wrinkles in the horizontal plane can indicate that a fast, all-purpose sail is getting good and flat for the heavy conditions at hand. In contrast, wrinkles that radiate at more than a 45-degree angle to the boom are detrimental to boat speed.

Luff sag affects the headsail in much the same way that mast bend affects the mainsail. Increasing headstay tension reduces the amount of luff sag and flattens the sail. Having a system to tighten the headstay is a must on any racing boat (if the rules allow it) because pointing ability increases with more headstay tension.

Move draft position forward. You should move the mainsail's draft position forward as the breeze picks up because the draft tends to move aft with increased wind strength. Tensioning the luff causes the amount of draft to either decrease or stay the same. If the position of maximum draft is moved forward, the after part of the sail - the portion behind the point of maximum draft - becomes much flatter. The result is a straighter exit off the leech, which depowers the sail and also allows the sheeting to be farther off the centerline. If the jib is sheeted farther off the centerline, it deflects less wind toward the mainsail, and the mainsail can be sheeted farther outboard.

Increase twist. Twist is the difference in trim angle between the top and the bottom of the sail; increased twist depowers the sail. In heavy winds, mainsail twist produces better pointing ability; the bottom of the sail is kept near the centerline to maintain weather helm, while the top of the sail is twisted off centerline to reduce the heeling force. Increasing twist in the sails works best in flat water; in a sea, the upper leech is needed to produce acceleration power.

Most racing boats have adjustable jib-lead systems because the jib-lead position is so important for controlling twist. You should begin to depower as the breeze comes up by increasing headsail twist. Moving the jib lead aft is usually sufficient on a dinghy. On an offshore boat, the jib lead is moved aft in a puff, and the sheet is trimmed in quickly so pointing ability is maintained.

Move sails off centerline. Moving sails off centerline is similar to increasing twist except that the entire sail, rather than just the top, moves to leeward. It's a good way to depower when: increasing or maintaining speed is more important than pointing; sea conditions are rough and constant acceleration through the waves is needed; or the boat is planing and needs to be depowered while staying on a plane.

The best way to ease a mainsail off centerline is to drop the traveler. If a puff hits, ease the traveler to lessen heeling; once the sails are depowered, bring the traveler back up to windward to maintain pointing ability.

Many dinghies use vang sheeting to move the main off centerline as an alternative to keeping the mainsheet tight and playing the traveler. The vang keeps the boom from lifting, and the mainsheet controls the distance of the boom off centerline. Dinghy sailors usually prefer vang sheeting because the boom is more quickly adjusted with the mainsheet.

In-and-out adjustment of the jib during a puff is less critical. Most dinghies and smaller boats have an optimal sheeting angle for the jib, and the increase in speed that results from moving the lead farther outboard does not seem to make up for the lack of pointing ability. For this reason, it's better to depower the jib by moving the lead aft and increasing twist.

Offshore boats, however, do move the genoa lead farther off centerline to depower, usually by attaching two sheets to the jib and putting more tension on the outboard sheet. Recently, some boats have had good success with athwartships genoa tracks; they make it easy to ease the lead off centerline in a puff and also control headsail twist by using an adjustable floating block attached to the track. The jib-lead angle is effectively moved aft by easing the block upward.

Two additional depowering techniques are used on many boats; increasing sidebend and adding mast rake (Fig. 2). Increased sidebend is more properly called windward sidebend because the boat depowers only if the middle of the mast bends to windward.

Create windward sidebend.   Windward sidebend – I don't recommend it for a masthead rig – can depower a fractional rig in heavy air by opening the slot between the mainsail and the jib, forcing the mast tip to fall off to leeward. The hounds act as a pivot, or fulcrum, with the tip section moving to leeward and the midsection moving to windward.

On an offshore boat, windward bend can be increased by loosening the upper shrouds, tightening the lower or intermediate shrouds, or both. Since headstay tension is controlled by adjustable backstays, headstay sag can be avoided by increasing backstay tension.

Shrouds cannot be eased on a dinghy without creating a lot of jib sag, so getting the right amount of sidebend in a dinghy requires achieving a balance among rig tension, spreader length, vang tension, boom position, and the bending characteristics of the mast section. The concept, though, is that when the vang is on firmly and the boom is trimmed close to the centerline, the mast should not bend to windward. But as the mainsheet is eased down and the boom goes off centerline, the pull that the mainsail leech exerts on the mast tip should pull the spar to leeward. The bending pivots about the hounds, forces the middle of the spar to windward, and opens the slot.

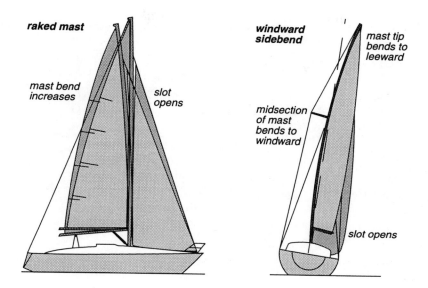

Fig. 2   *If your rig can be adjusted so the mast tip can sag off to leeward and depower the main, the mast will bend to windward at its midsection, opening up the slot. Increasing mast rake improves heavy-air speed to windward.*

You should watch the spar to make sure that sidebend is increasing as the mainsheet is eased. Overly long spreaders or too much rig tension can prevent sidebend. Because reducing rig tension sacrifices headstay tension, it is preferable to shorten the spreaders, if allowable under your class or handicap rules, until the desired bending is achieved. However, don't shorten the spreaders more than necessary; sidebend will occur too early, and the boat won't have enough power for medium wind conditions. Remember, too, that boom vang tension is a key element because it creates the leech tension that bends the mast tip to leeward.

Add mast rake.   Adding rake is a depowering technique that works well on small boats and is also proving to be fast on most offshore boats. Adding rake has a number of benefits:

- The sailplan is lowered, taking some of the sail area out of the stronger wind above the surface of the water, where there is less surface friction.

- The slot is opened as the mainsail moves farther away from the jib.
- Mast bend is increased unless the spar is stepped on deck or the partners are adjusted when rake is added.
- The sailplan's center of effort is moved aft. This point is critical because if the helm is unbalanced, adding rake will slow your boat down.

These depowering techniques will work with varying degrees of success, on all boats; any or all of them can be appropriate once the breeze picks up. If you know how each can help you depower your sails, you can choose the right combinations for the conditions you are facing.

III

Cruising Trim

Light-Air Sail Power

*Sometimes even cruising sailors
need trim help*

Lin and Larry Pardey

Most cruisers are more concerned with gale tactics than light-air performance. Yet light winds predominate along many cruising routes. If you can keep your boat moving under sail, you'll be able to reach remote destinations instead of determining your route by refueling ports.

Long-distance cruising boats have three special – and major – problems. First, the majority are overweight. Second, they are short of crew. Last, they usually carry a limited inventory of "luxury" sails, such as light-air headsails. Overcoming these handicaps calls for a combination of design improvements, good sail choice, and sailing tactics.

Design considerations. Although a boat's potential speed in light air is most accurately calculated by comparing the amount of wetted surface (hull below the waterline) with sail area, we've come up with the following rule of thumb. Divide total displacement (designed weight plus 1,500 pounds per person aboard) by 2,000 pounds to get short tonnage. Divide working sail area (the total of the mainsail and 100 percent of the foretriangle) by the tonnage. If the resulting figure is much less than about 83 square feet per ton, you'll find it difficult to set the light canvas required to keep your boat moving in light airs. A light-air flyer might carry 110 square feet of working sail area per ton – 132 square feet per ton with a 150 percent genoa. Our old boat, *Seraffyn,* carried 88 square feet of working sail area per ton, 127 feet with her big genoa. Figures for our current boat, 29-foot, 6-inch *Taleisin,* are similar.

The full sections of classic long-keel hulls, plus the inherent momentum of a heavier displacement, are often positive contributions to light-air performance. Fuller-bodied hulls can actually present less wetted surface for their displacement than do many flat-bottomed, fin-keeled racer/cruisers. The additional weight, if combined with a good spread of canvas, helps keep the boat moving between puffs of wind. So, contrary to popular belief, these older designs, such as 1950s CCA boats, RORC-inspired hulls, and classics like Cape Dorys, often perform better than more contemporary designs in light airs.

Propeller configuration also affects light-air performance. In winds below 10 knots, a day's run can be increased by around four percent with a two-blade folding prop as compared with a two-blade fixed prop. Three-blade solid props, although they are more fuel-efficient and possibly smoother running under power, are even more costly in terms of boat speed.

Racers know that a clean bottom is essential for successful light-air performance and choose hard bottom paints that can be scrubbed down before each race. For offshore voyagers, an acceptable compromise is a leaching bottom paint designed to be wiped off by a snorkeler three or four times between haulouts.

A clear deck also helps in light air. A clutter of bicycles, water jugs, spray shields, and dodgers causes wind drag. Also, to handle light-air sails, you will need to move around on the side decks and the foredeck. The clearer these areas are, the easier and safer sail handling will be.

The "right" light-air sail. The "right" light-air sail is easy to set and control and capable of being used all around the wind rose. If light-air sails are difficult to handle, many of us take the cockeyed optimist's approach: "If I wait a bit, the wind will freshen." Meanwhile, we curse the slatting jib or start the engine.

After trying a variety of light-wind sails, we've found the most versatile is our 540-square-foot nylon drifter. It is cut from 1.2-ounce nylon and is the same size as our #1 genoa, but with a higher clew. It can be set flying (i.e., no hanks) on its own low-stretch Kevlar-cored luff rope, but it also has four jib hanks spaced equally along its luff. Unlike the typical asymmetric cruising spinnaker, this flat-cut sail can be used for going to windward in about five knots of apparent wind; we use the hanks to help hold the luff tight. Twenty degrees farther off the wind, we unhank the sail and set it flying. We carry it downwind in up to 15 knots of breeze or until its 1/4-inch diameter sheets start to get skinny.

Unlike spinnakers or cruising chutes, a drifter does not chafe against the headstay in sloppy conditions, nor does it have the same tendency to wrap around the forestay in fluky wind. Our drifter weighs only 15 pounds and can easily be stuffed into a space the size of a five-gallon pail.

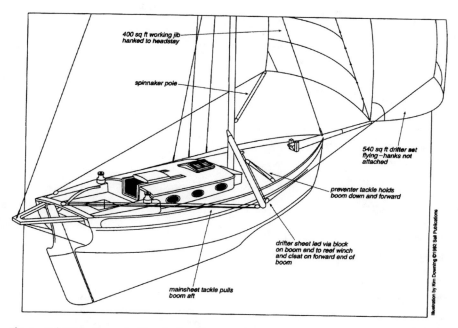

Fig. 1 Taleisin's *downwind headsail configuration. The working jib and drifter are easily handled individually.*

In winds above 10 knots we usually run wing-and-wing with our 100 percent lapper set on a whisker pole opposite the mainsail. As the wind drops, we get out the drifter and set it flying to leeward (Fig. 1). Its sheet is led to a block seized to the outhaul fitting of the mainsail boom. From there the sheet leads to the jiffy-reefing winch and reefing-pennant cleats at the mast. Since the drifter's sheet and halyard are right at the mast, setting and lowering the sail is a one-person job. To steady the drifter, we push the boom forward and use a preventer tackle to hold it in place. The boom thus works as a drifter pole. Once the drifter is set, we drop the mainsail into the lazyjacks.

The two headsails – jib on its pole, drifter on the main boom – give us almost as much sail area as we'd carry with a symmetrical spinnaker and more than we'd have with an asymmetric chute (Fig. 2), but with much more versatility. If the wind falls light or the sea gets lumpy and the Dacron jib starts to slat or bang, we drop it and use only the drifter. If the wind freshens as we're running wing-and-wing, it's easy to douse the larger sail,

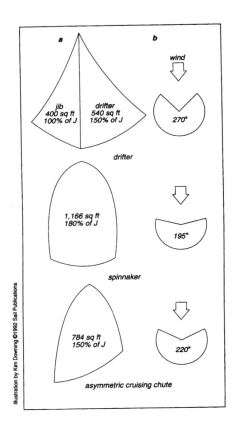

Illustration by Kim Downing ©1992 Sail Publications

Fig. 2 *Comparative areas (a) for different headsails for a 38-foot boat with an I measurement (hoist) of 40 feet and a J (base of foretriangle) of 18 feet. The drifter-jib combination is not as efficient aerodynamically, but is more manageable and has ample area. (b) Usable range of wind angles for three headsail types.*

the drifter. We just hoist the mainsail (ours has no headboard or battens so can normally be raised on any point of wind), ease the spinnaker halyard, and gather in the billowing expanse of nylon in the lee of the mainsail. If the wind shifts forward and remains light, we can drop the jib and its whisker pole, sheet in the main boom and drifter, and set the mainsail, so we're properly canvassed for beam-reaching or going to windward later.

Cost.   When cost determines your sail choices, the combination of a drifter opposite a 100 percent jib represents the thrifty way to gain sail area downwind. The snuffers often used with a spinnaker or asymmetric chute seem to us expensive and bulky. We think they sometimes fail to work properly in the rougher conditions found offshore, and worse, they can cause chafe at the head of your sail. By dividing your downwind rig into two headsails, you end up with a drifter that can be handled easily without special containment gear.

Furling jibs are built to cover a wide range of winds, so sailmakers usually choose heavier fabric than normal and then add a layer of sun-protection cloth along the foot and leech of the sail. This produces poor light-air performance. The cost of carrying a light-weather furling genoa, plus the difficulty of changing from one furling headsail to another, could mean you'll just roll up the jib and power.

Mainsails. Mainsails are usually cut from fabric that is too heavy to work well in light breezes, especially in choppy seas. The bang/slat of even the most tightly vanged and prevented mainsail can wake a sound sleeper. When we are trying to cross seas leftover from a 20-knot beam wind with a light wind behind us, we find it best to drop the mainsail and rely completely on quiet nylon chafe-free headsails.

Full-batten mainsails have been suggested as a solution to light-air sailing. But the cost of universal-joint batten cars to make sure the sail goes up and down properly, the common problem of batten-pocket chafe, and the difficulty of raising and lowering the sail at any time other than when you are head-to-wind make us feel this type of mainsail is too expensive for the trade-off of larger roach area, less chance of luffing, and stowing simplicity.

Sailing in light air. To keep a boat moving in light zephyrs it is important to try anything properly that will keep the sails still and shaped to catch the wind. Inducing a slight heel, either by getting the crew to lounge or sleep on the leeward side or by moving a few water jugs to leeward, will help. Using a vang to hold the mainsail out and down so it doesn't pump the wind out on each swell is important, both on the wind and running. Going downwind in very light breezes, it pays to wing the jib out snugly and, if necessary, put a downhaul on the whisker pole to steady it. A smaller 100 percent headsail, which can be held square on the pole, will work better in these conditions than a 150 percent genoa that undulates and curls.

A racing tactic that pays dividends in light-air cruising is avoiding running dead downwind unless the breeze is fresh and steady. By reaching up about 20 degrees, even if it is off your rhumb line, you'll keep the boat moving better, you'll cover a little extra ground but will make an overall faster passage. The boat will stay steadier, and the speed gain will be substantial, with less risk of an accidental gybe.

Going upwind on a laden cruising boat in light air, you'll find it pays to keep off the true wind after you tack – to "let it breathe." Instead of pinching right up, let the boat off five degrees more than you would in fresher winds. Get the boat moving and trimmed on this easy-breathing course, then slowly work closer to the wind, sheeting the sails in inch by inch. Again, slightly more ground to cover, but a faster passage.

Most other axioms for light-air racing apply to light-air cruising. Ease the halyards and outhaul tension slightly on all sails so there are slight wrinkles but no puckers along the luff or foot. This gives your sails a fuller, more powerful shape. Ease the mainsheet a bit to relieve any weather helm so the rudder can be kept aligned with the keel to cut down on drag. If your boat develops lee helm, as many do under large headsails in light winds, sheet the mainsail in a bit extra. Steer to traverse the seas instead of heading directly into leftover swells or chop, and ease the sheets to keep the boat moving. Over the long distances of a passage, you'll soon make up for any course deviations.

Light-air sailing may be an acquired taste for those who cruise close to home. But for those who eventually visit far-off shores, 60 to 70 miles a day for free can look pretty good. Carrying the right equipment and learning the tactics will make light-air days a rewarding part of your voyage.

A New Approach: The Maxi-Roach

Too much is sometimes just enough

Steve Dashew

██████████████

Would you like to make a quantum leap in your cruising performance? Does your conservative cruising rig leave you wallowing in the wake of your more highly powered neighbors? If the answer to either of these questions is yes, read on.

Your sails generate lift and drag. To improve performance you must reduce drag and/or increase lift. In most cases, within a fixed set of rig parameters, there's little you can do toward this end.

Of the various forms of drag your sails generate, induced drag is the easiest to reduce. Induced drag is the downwind component of the force embodying aerodynamic lift. The difference in pressure between the two sides of the sail causes air to try to flow from the high-pressure side (windward) to the low-pressure side (leeward). Flow around the foot and head of the sail results in spiraling vortexes. These, in effect, suck energy away from the sail. Minimum induced drag is developed by an elliptically shaped sail.

Lowering induced drag means the sail might achieve adequate lift at a lower angle of attack – that is, you could sail closer to the wind, in a more upright fashion, and faster. Short of replacing your entire rig with a taller, more efficient spar section and putting on a deeper-draft keel, there has been little you could do.

On the other hand, boat speed in light-to-medium air is pretty much a function of sail area. More area equals more drive, and as long as you're not overcome by heeling, more sail area is better.

In the last 10 years, as the full-batten mainsail (and mizzen) has come of age, I've seen dramatic proof that reducing drag by increasing sail area and making the sail plan more efficient improves boat performance. In six cases I've been directly involved with, hollow leech mainsails have been replaced with full-batten, slightly roached sails. The 10 percent increase in sail area has improved speed, but more surprising have been the other results; I think I have actually seen less heel and reduced weather helm.

When I asked John Letcher, a highly experienced aero/hydro-dynamicist from Southwest Harbor, Maine, about our observed results, he wasn't completely skeptical. "The closer you can get to an elliptical shape, the better off you're going to be." What we'd observed with the added roach area was an effective step toward an elliptical mainsail plan.

Peter Schwenn of Design Systems, Annapolis, Maryland, added that "The extra area, up high, works better because the wind is stronger aloft." He thought that a bigger, more efficiently shaped sail could conceivably result in a boat that points higher and sails faster, at a lower heel angle, most likely by offering better speed in lighter wind. For an equal wind strength, more speed and less heel would be very hard to achieve.

More is better.   If a small amount of roach is good, is a lot better? In my opinion, the answer is a definite yes. More roach gets you closer to an elliptical sail plan (less drag), with more sail area up high (Fig. 1). Open-class racing dinghies and catamarans (and now the International America's Cup class) have shown this for years.

The problem with most cruising rigs, however, is that the permanent backstay that is needed to support the mast gets in the way of an optimum sail shape. Some sails, including the mizzen on our 67-foot ketch, *Sundeer*, overlap their backstays, but this overlap has usually been just a couple of inches. Many transoceanic single-handed racers, both mono- and multihull, have large roach overlaps, but since they have to tack only infrequently, the skipper lowers the main when turning through the wind.

With the above facts in mind, I sat down with John Conser of Wind-ward Sails in Costa Mesa, California, to design a new mainsail for my father's 74-foot cutter. Sail plan in hand, I told John we wanted as much roach as possible. The two of us reckoned we could sneak three or four inches of the sail past the backstay. That would increase the area of the sail almost eight percent compared with the normal roach, and, given the boat's very conservative mast height, it could use every bit of area we could add.

You can imagine how John, my dad, and I felt when four weeks later the new mainsail was hoisted. Instead of jutting just a few inches past the backstay, the sail overlapped by 28 inches! The combination of a dimen-

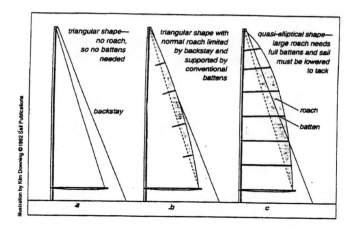

Fig. 1   *The basic mainsail shape is triangular, not an inherently efficient shape aerodynamically. On roller-furling mains, there is even less area, because the leech much be cut slightly hollow. The most common mainsail shape is still mainly triangular, but with as much roach as the backstay allows. The quasi-elliptical mainsail comes closest to the optimum aerodynamic form for a high lift-to-drag ratio.*

sional error on my part and a computer mistake on John's had led to this fateful moment.

The sail looked very sexy, and a quick calculation showed that if a way could be found to use the sail (doubtful), we'd end up adding 12 percent to the total area of the rig. We were after horsepower, but this was a bit extreme.

As we sailed out of the harbor in light air, we could feel the increased power and speed. For most of the afternoon we dropped the main a couple of feet on the halyard each time we tacked and gybed. Obviously, this wasn't going to work other than for testing. As the time approached to head back, I asked my dad to let us try a series of tacks and gybes without dropping the main. "Just for fun, let's see what happens."

You can imagine our surprise, and then delight, as the overlap paused and then cleared the backstay in just 3 to 4 knots of wind. John and I looked at each other as the impact started to sink in. If we could work out the details, we might just have a quantum leap in performance.

When we returned to the dock, we examined the leech of the sail. It had suffered a bit of chafe from the backstay where the battens rubbed. Otherwise everything looked fine.

Photographs by Steve Dashew

Photo 1   *Same boat, same rig, but look at the difference in main and mizzen areas before (small photo) and after (large photo). The addition is worth up to 10 percent in boat speed, says the author.*

The next day, in 10 to 12 knots of wind, we went out again. Not only were we sailing 7 to 10 percent faster upwind compared with the old main, it even seemed that the boat was heeling several degrees less and that weather helm was reduced. The more efficient shape also allowed us to point higher.

Conser has since made similar sails for *Sundeer* (Photo 1) and for the 62-foot cutter *Moonshadow*. Aboard *Sundeer* we took careful before-and-after measurements with a Brookes & Gatehouse Hercules 390 instrument system, including a set of polar tables predicting performance at various wind strengths and angles. By this more objective but still tentative indicator, our downwind performance polars were up 8 to 11 percent, while upwind speed improved slightly less. Even though we added almost 17 percent to our mainsail area, we felt our wind range to the first reef could be increased by two knots.

How much overlap?   Just how much roach overlap you could add depends on a series of factors. First, the more distance between the end of your boom and the backstay, the more area you'll be able to add. With a lot of older cruising designs this can be very significant.

Also, a decision needs to be made about the lowest wind speed in which you want the sail to clear the backstay (if you race, it's half a knot; if you cruise, it's the wind speed at which you turn on the engine).

For *Sundeer's* mainsail I decided that I didn't want to reef to tack in anything above five knots of wind. We designed a maximum overlap equal to about 20 percent of the distance between the mast and the backstay where the greatest overlap occurs. So, with a dimension of 9.5 feet from the mast to the backstay, we added two feet of roach beyond the backstay (Fig. 2).

Only experience can yield optimum results. However, there's something to be said for adding as much as you think prudent, since it's always possible to cut roach off but impossible to add it.

Dealing with chafe. To minimize chafe from the backstay, we experimented with a number of different approaches. In the end it was the simple methods that worked best.

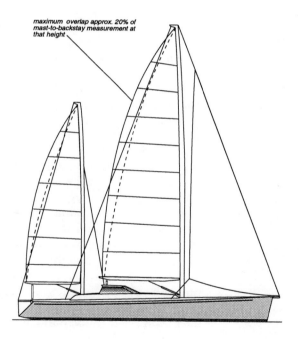

maximum overlap approx. 20% of mast-to-backstay measurement at that height

Fig. 2 Sundeer's *sail plan shows the extent of the roach additions in relation to the original main and mizzen.*

We used a length of one-inch-diameter PVC tube as long as the over-lapping portion of the roach. Slipped over the upper portion of the backstay and resting on a hose clamp tightened around the stay, the pipe acts as a roller bearing that both eases the sail's passage during tacks and minimizes chafe.

To protect the sailcloth, a four-inch strip of 1/16-inch-thick ultra high-molecular weight plastic was sewn over the batten pockets where they overlap the backstay (Photo 2). The UHMW/PVC combination allows the sail to blow by the backstay in relatively light air.

Batten considerations. The upper battens are significantly longer than those in a standard sail, so they need to be stiffer than you might otherwise use. However, as the sail passes the backstay, the battens are deflected substantially, so they shouldn't be too stiff (Photo 3). Finding the correct batten stiffness is a function of trial and error. In the end, they should be just stiff enough to support the roach when the sail is reefed down, and no more.

We've ended up using solid, round-section, pultruded fiberglass battens made with vinylester resin. The vinylester bends farther than polyester without failing. Incidentally, the longer top battens project farther aft past the lazyjacks and are less likely to foul them than the old battens, a big plus when raising or lowering the sail.

Tacking and gybing. We've been cruising with these big-roach sails now for some time and have found a couple of tricks for tacking and gybing. Upwind, if the main is trimmed hard, it is necessary to ease the sheet a touch as we come through the eye of the wind. The lighter the air, the more we ease the sheet.

Gybing in anything over five knots of apparent wind goes smoothly. In winds lighter than that, it is necessary to make sure the boom is accelerated as it comes across, either by swinging the helm a little quicker than normal, by giving the sheet a good tug, or by pushing on the boom.

In very light air, when the main won't clear quickly and maneuvering room is at a premium, we drop it to the first deep reef. Then the sail blows through easily. At this point we have the

Photo 2   *Battens are protected against backstay chafe with tough, ultrahigh-molecular-weight plastic patches.*

same sail area as with the old, small-roach sails and can sail all day in tight places.

There is absolutely nothing you can do to an older cruising boat that will increase performance as much as a maxi-roach mainsail, regardless of how much money you're prepared to spend. What's the risk? Not much. If you give this concept a try and find it doesn't fit your cruising concept, your sailmaker can reduce the roach with a minimum of effort. But once you feel the power that comes from one of these sails, the odds of your cutting it back are pretty slim.

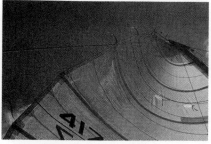

Photographs by Steve Dashew

Photo 3   *Here's what tacking the mainsail looks like from* Sundeer's *deck. A couple of years of sailing proves it works, but maybe it's better not to watch.*

Your Deck Layout Makes All the Difference

Simplified cruising decks work best

Wally Cross

Many of the boats I see, both cruisers and racers, have far more deck hardware than they need. This is due mainly to the outdated idea that more hardware made sailing easier.

Today, most sailors and designers agree less is best. To get an idea of contemporary layouts for a cruising boat and a racing boat, look at the deck plans in Figures 1 and 2.

Control lines. All the lines you need for sail control, except those for sheet trimming and headsail furling, should be led aft from the mast to a central area on the cabinhouse. Leading these lines to a central point, referred to by racing crews as the "pit," is the first step in making crew work easier.

Two self-tailing winches, one on each side of the house, can handle up to six halyard and adjustment lines, as long as those lines are run through a device called a sheet stopper or jammer. There are a variety of jammers on the market today. Most do a great job of stopping off the halyards and also allow them to be released easily when under a load. "Jammed off" is the phrase used for cleating or, in this case, jamming a line before taking the strain off the winch.

Just behind the row of jammers should be an "organizer" – a series of sheaves that allow each line to lead smoothly from its jammer to either the port or the starboard winch. This combination of jammers and an orga-

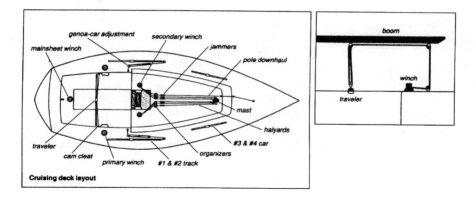

Fig. 1 *A good cruising setup leads halyards and spinnaker lines through a halyard stopper and organizer system. A good plan is to locate the traveler in the after part of the cockpit, with a block at the end of the boom and the mainsheet winch nearby. The car's position is adjusted from the outboard ends of the traveler. Traveler arrangements vary considerably; many are positioned on the cabinhouse, with the mainsheet winch near the traveler.*

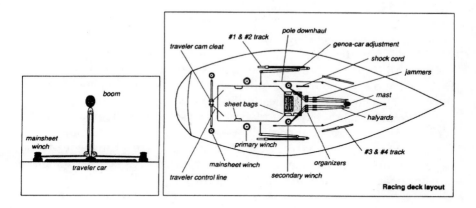

Fig. 2 *A racing layout places two self-tailing winches, one on each side of the cabinhouse, to handle halyards and sail-adjustment lines through a system of halyard stoppers and an organizer. The traveler should be located as far aft as possible; the configuration includes a double-ended mainsheet with winches for adjusting the sheet located at each end of the traveler. Traveler adjustment can be made most easily at the traveler car.*

nizer allows you to have just two winches. The key is placing the winches so all the lines lead cleanly to them from the organizer.

This layout can work for the grand prix racer, the club racer, and the well-appointed cruiser. A racing boat should have the main halyard, two or three jib halyards, the spinnaker pole lift, the cunningham, and probably the boom vang running through jammers and the organizer. A good cruising setup should have the main halyard, roller-furling genoa halyard, cruising spinnaker halyard, spinnaker pole downhaul, boom vang adjustment, reefing lines and pole lift for the whisker pole running through the system. Some cruising boats even run the halyard for the forestaysail through a jammer.

With all these lines coming into the pit area, there is a risk that they may become tangled and snarled. If you put sheet bags on either side of the companionway or cockpit to hold the loose line tails, they will most likely not turn into a bowl of spaghetti.

Some race boats are starting to use a shock-cord arrangement on the deck. Basically, it's a piece of cord that runs between two small fittings, but the cord can keep a spinnaker halyard, or any halyard that needs to be released quickly, clear of the rest of the lines. This arrangement works just as well on a cruising boat.

A racing boat setup should also include a double-ended spinnaker pole downhaul whose ends lead aft along each side of the cabinhouse. A cruising boat should always have the lead for the roller-furling headsail system running all the way aft. The line should be led well clear of other deck gear so it can't get tangled.

Genoa adjustments.   All boats benefit from having an adjustable car mechanism. A pair of primary genoa tracks should handle the #1 and #2 headsails, and a secondary pair – up forward by the shrouds – should handle the #3 and smaller #4 and #5 headsails, if the boat carries them.

Primary tracks seem to work best when set at eight degrees from the centerline on a racing boat and at 10 degrees on a modern cruising boat. I find that #3 and #4 genoas trim best when the track is set at an angle of nine degrees from the centerline for a race boat; 13 degrees is good for most cruising boats. Obviously, these angles can vary, especially on cruising boats. If you have doubts about what angle is best, consult your sailmaker before you start making changes.

Adjustable genoa car systems have become very popular. They make it simple to move the lead position for the jib clew fore and aft on the track by pulling on a single line. Racing sailors use the system to change the shape of the sail when wind conditions change. Cruising sailors, particularly those whose boats have roller-furling genoas, can move the cars quickly whenever sail area is changed by rolling or unrolling.

For example, if the headsail is rolled up because of increasing wind velocity, the foot of the sail becomes shorter. That means the lead must be moved forward to keep the sail working at maximum efficiency and the helm properly balanced.

Good ball-bearing cars keep friction to a minimum, so a smaller purchase is needed to move the car under load. A boat up to 40 feet should have a minimum four-to-one purchase, while for a boat over 40 feet six-to-one is better.

Travelers.   Although traveler designs vary slightly, all travelers do the same job – control the shape of the mainsail and vary its position relative to the apparent wind. Here again, the key is to have a good ball-bearing traveler car that slides smoothly and can be adjusted easily under load.

There's only one major difference between a traveler setup for a cruising boat and one used for racing. On a cruising boat the control lines should cleat at the outboard ends of the traveler. A racing crew is better off having the control line adjustment at a traveler car.

Finally, there are mainsheets. A racing mainsheet should be set up a little differently from a cruising one. Racing boats up to 40 feet should use a block-and-tackle mainsheet system (six-to-one), and those over 40 feet should use a winching system with a double-ended mainsheet and two winches, each winch located just outboard of either end of the traveler.

The same six-to-one block-and-tackle system is fine for a cruising boat up to 40 feet. Over 40 feet, the block-and-tackle system, with a single winch amidships somewhere near the traveler, is a good solution.

Next spring take a look around your deck. See if your setup reflects some of the ideas I've mentioned here. Today's thinking is that the easier your boat is to sail, the more enjoyable it will be for you and your crew.

Twin Headstays for Cruising

You can cruise for days, pulled by this easy sail arrangement

Steve Dashew

<hr/>

Twin headstays, once considered only in the context of bluewater passagemaking, are finding their way aboard more coastal cruisers. The versatility and sailhandling ease they offer in tradewind areas can be even more valuable in the variable winds you might find closer to home. A properly set up twin headstay system gives you two different sails, with differing sizes and cloth weights, ready to go. If you're on a light beat with a large genoa and the wind comes up, changing down to a comfortable #3 is quick and easy, especially when you're shorthanded.

Twin headstays mounted side by side originally evolved for use in the tradewinds. Identical poled-out jibs were used as an aid to self-steering and to eliminate gybe-related damage to the mainsail. The main would be set, perhaps with a deep reef, to reduce the rhythmic rolling usually induced by the poled headsails.

Our own experience in various tradewind belts has taught my wife, Linda, and me that a stable, never-changing wind doesn't exist. As a result, you are always trying to alter sail size and trim. With jibs poled out, that is a limited option.

The advent of powerful self-steering devices has eliminated the need to have identical twin headsails. At the same time, rig size has grown in proportion to boat size, making sail changing more difficult for shorthanded crews. If you can combine twin headsails with the possibility of using roller furling, they begin to make even more sense.

My first experience with twin headstays began after a refit of our 50-foot ketch, *Intermezzo*; the boat had then covered 10,000 miles of the Pacific with a single headstay and conventional staysail stay. *Intermezzo* was a bit tender, and we found that we were changing headsails up and down quite often to keep her moving comfortably in the changing wind. After pulling the spar for inspection, we decided to add a second headstay just aft of the principal headstay. To do so, we put a second set of tangs on the mast between the staysail stay and the headstay attachment points.

Since the new stay position would induce an eccentric bending load in the upper section of the mast, we made attachment points on the mast and fabricated longer pennants for our running backstays so they could be used higher up to steady the mast.

For good downwind and reaching performance, we placed the light #1 genoa on the outer headstay. When the breeze started to come up, we dropped the #1 in favor of the #3 jib, now bent on its own inner headstay. While we could be slightly under-canvassed with the #3 at first, it was a convenient way to change down. At the worst, we lost 0.3 knot in the lower range of the #3. Once the wind got up to around 15 knots, the boat would sail smartly.

Off the wind, we found that we could set the outer, or windward, jib by taking the clew to the spinnaker pole; it could be carried as close to the wind as 90 degrees apparent. We would sheet the inner jib to leeward. It would stay filled even in an apparent wind of 160 degrees. With a full main, this was a powerful, easily handled rig that had the advantage of being able to sail through a wide range of conditions and make few demands on the crew. When off-the-wind conditions got very boisterous, we would put the larger jib away and sail with the smaller one poled out to windward.

When we were sailing in an area where there was a good chance of foul weather, we would attach the staysail stay to its normal place on deck and coil the inner headstay into the forepeak, along with the long backstay pennants. We would then put the #3 jib on the outer stay, giving the mast better support in case we encountered bad conditions.

Jim and Cheryl Schmidt had another approach to twin headstays on their Deerfoot 70, *Wakaroa*. They had #1 and #3 genoas set on separate roller-furling stays. In *Wakaroa*'s case, the stays were quite close together both at the masthead and at the bow, so special support from runners wasn't required.

The only negative was that they had to roll up the outer sail both to tack and to gybe; in contrast, our outer headsail would clear the inner one when we tacked, albeit slowly. When tacking was required going to windward, they used the inner genoa. On the plus side, they had a wider range of efficient usage between the two sails. They still had a removable staysail stay, with runners, for setting a storm staysail.

.   The Schmidt's twin headstay approach can be used on boats down to 35 feet. Though roller furling is required on the outer headstay, using it on both the inner and the outer stay gives the widest range of sail combinations with minimum crew exertion. Both headsails can be set downwind with the main, and jib size can be chosen with ease for sailing across the wind.

For our second *Intermezzo*, a stiff 62-footer, I was most concerned with being able to change headsails up or down in heavy weather with ease, but without roller furling. This time I opted for twin headstays placed side by side. My theory was that I would have two different-sized headsails hanked on in the high latitudes, both could be quickly hoisted or doused, and both could be tacked through the foretriangle area without hanging up on another stay.

To reduce the chance of having the hanks on one stay foul the other sail, the stays were placed 12 inches apart at the deck and six inches apart at the masthead. Because this wide spacing would induce a twisting force at the masthead, we also installed twin backstays to counteract the problem.

My next concern was running and broad-reaching conditions. While I was still not a big fan of twin jibs that were set on poles, I felt it would be nice to have a cruising spinnaker made with hanks so it could be flown off the leeward stay. We have flown this sail to leeward, with the genoa set on the pole to windward, for many thousands of miles and have had excellent results. The system is easy to handle and gives us a powerful but controlled sailplan.

There are a couple of drawbacks to side-by-side headstays. The first is headstay sag. The static backstay tension you put into the rig at the dock is divided between both headstays. This means that either stay will sag more than if all the backstay tension were going into a single stay. As the wind picks us, greater headstay sag results in a more fully shaped jib, which is precisely what you don't want in those conditions. The headsail luff can be hollowed out more than usual by the sailmaker to compensate for the extra sag, but then a problem arises in light air: When the stay is tight, the sails may be too flat.

The second problem has to do with chafe. If you set a headsail on the weather stay, and you're sailing a bit free, the luff on that sail will rub back and forth across the leeward headstay. This is hard on the seam stitching.

The best cure is to have a long chafe patch attached to both sides of any headsail that may suffer the problem.

Our 62-footer has covered more than 10,000 miles with this twin headstay system and has not suffered from either interlocking hanks or hanks jumping from one stay to another. Some of our cruising friends with side-by-side twins haven't been so lucky. In fact, they consider these problems to be a fairly common occurrence. If the stays are set closer together or you sail a boat having a bit of headstay sag, the annoyance is something with which you must live.

For his third circumnavigation with the 56-foot *Islander*, Tom Blackwell did away with conventional hanks. He opted instead to shackle his headsails to their respective stays. If you have enough freeboard forward to carry the unused headsail secured on deck without fear of damage in heavy going, this approach makes some sense.

Should twin headstays have a place aboard your cruising boat? If your passages are routinely longer than the short-hop variety, or if you sail in an area with very changeable conditions, I would suggest looking at them very closely. From our own experience, I would use a fore-and-aft twin system on boats from 35 to 50 feet – or wherever roller furling seems to make good sense. At the point in boat size where you want to be able to carry, and tack easily, two different sizes of headsails without roller furling, then you should consider installing side-by-side twins. Obviously, in order for side-by-side stays to be effective, you must have a rig and boat that will take high static loading on the headstay.

Remember a few more things when you are thinking of rigging twins. First, be very careful of eccentric loads in the mast, and check with the mast manufacturer first. At a minimum, twin backstays or runners may be required. Also be sure you know how the loads are distributed onto the fittings on the deck. Here again, the potential for eccentric loads must be assessed carefully. If you are planning on making long passages, your headsail luffs should have vertical chafe patches applied to them.

But even with these extra words of caution, I think twin headstays are worth looking at. In fact, look at them even if you are only planning to go cruising alongshore.

Mastering the Running Backstay

Here are ways to control new mast types

Steve Cruse

With the trend toward higher performance in today's cruiser-racers, quite a few features that originated in grand prix racing are appearing on production boats. One good example is the mast, which has become smaller in section to reduce windage and weight aloft. These newer, more slender mast sections are inherently more willing to bend than the older "tree-trunk" type, and consequently need more support to keep them straight and to prevent them from pumping in a seaway.

As a result, many masts come equipped with running backstays. And, not surprisingly, a growing number of sailors are wondering how to use these backstays properly. In very general terms, running backstays, or runners, are there to steady the mast. But, depending on the design of the rig, they can be used quite differently. To show you what I mean, let's look at the first of four basic arrangements that can be found on contemporary rigs.

You should know at the outset that running backstays have been around for a long time. In fact, they have been in and out of vogue several times over the past 50 years. They owe their most recent absence on most rigs to the stiffness of the aluminum mast that replaced overly flexible wooden spars in the late 1950s. Running backstays are still fairly common on cutter rigs, though, because they offset the bending moment caused by the loading of the inner forestay when the staysail is set.

The running backstays are attached to the aft side of the spar on either side of the mainsail track and generally directly opposite the inner forestay attachment. If all the sails are set, the windward runner should be set up using a moderate amount of tension to keep the mast straight and in column and, at the same time, to reduce the sag of the inner forestay.

I know many cruisers feel runners are a nuisance because their location on deck is such that every time you tack, the old windward runner must be eased off and the new windward runner tensioned. Not only that, the new leeward runner must be secured to keep it from banging against the leeward rigging. Actually, with the standard cruising rig, on all points of sail except a run, both runners can be led to alternate locations farther forward. Hook the runners to the forward location using a four-to-one purchase system with the lower end secured to a properly backed padeye on the deck. This arrangement gives you adequate mast support in light-to-moderate conditions and also keeps the runners out of the way of the mainsail on beats and reaches. However, if the wind and seas increase, you should move the windward runner aft to its original location to get better support for the mast and inner forestay.

Moving up the performance scale in rigs, you find what is perhaps the most common setup on today's very competitive mid-sized racer-cruiser. The fore-and-aft lower shrouds have been replaced by a single set of lowers that are placed in line with the mast and the upper shrouds. This configuration reduces both the weight and windage, provides a better sheeting arrangement for a modern #3 blade jib, and permits the mast to be intentionally bent in the fore-and-aft direction by adjusting tension on a permanent backstay or a babystay or both. The mast sections used on stock production boats with this arrangement are moderately proportioned and have good fore-and-aft stiffness in light-to-moderate airs.

On rigs of this type runners are necessary only when you need additional support in fresh winds or you are sailing in sea conditions that would create a fore-and-aft pumping motion in the center portion of the mast. In this case the runners should be tensioned just enough to stop the pumping. They must never be over-tensioned to the point where they cause an inversion, or a backwards bending in the mast. On a rig of this type runners are important but not crucial to the safety of the rig, so you don't have to worry about being precise if the boat you are thinking of buying has them installed.

A third type of rig has two running backstays on each side of the mast; the lower one is called the checkstay. This arrangement is found on state-of-the-art masthead rigs, such as the triple-spreader-rigged C&C 41. By carefully controlling the mast's fore-and-aft bend, the runners are used for mast support as well as for controlling mainsail shape. Runners with checkstays are used on tall and very supple mast sections that permit large amounts of mast bend when the permanent backstay and perhaps the babystay are tensioned.

When the rig is set up properly at the maststep and the mast partners, this type of mast section can develop more than enough fore-and-aft bend (when the permanent backstay is also tensioned) to create the correct mast setting for a given wind condition. The backstay is needed only to provide support to the lower mast when the compressive forces of a spinnaker pole are present. Otherwise, the babystay can be removed for faster tacking.

The runner and the checkstay, which are connected, should be tensioned to bring the amount of mast bend to the "desired" curve and to also provide the support necessary to eliminate pumping in a seaway. The correct amount of mast bend is the amount that gives you the optimum mainsail shape for the conditions. Generally, easing the runner creates more mast bend, which flattens the main, and tightening the runner straightens the mast and adds fullness. Whoever is trimming the running backstay never should be overzealous in fresh conditions and crank it in too hard. It certainly could cause an excessively full mainsail and might cause a mast inversion.

You should set up the checkstays with a fine-tune adjustment, perhaps a tackle system where the checkstay joins the runner or an adjustment system led internally through the mast to the deck. This adjustment should be independent of the runner to which it is mated.

One good rule of thumb is that when you sight up the mainsail from under the boom, the sail should have an even amount of draft along its full length. You can see this easily if you use draft stripes on the main. After you have set up the runners, if the upper draft stripe is flatter than the lower stripe, ease the checkstay a little. If the sail is fuller higher up, tension the checkstay a little. Once the draft curve is even at each stripe, the sail's overall fullness then can be adjusted by either tensioning or easing the main runner.

Finally, these backstay arrangements also may be found on fractional rigs. With a single-runner configuration, the windward runner provides the headstay tension and, therefore, headsail shape. Although the permanent backstay also provides some headstay support, it is used mainly for fine-tuning the mainsail.

A very high performance fractional rig includes runners and checkstays. On these rigs the permanent backstay does not provide any headstay tension at all because these masts are so flexible. The runner is totally responsible for headstay tension, and therefore it should be hooked up to a powerful tackle or winch. Here again, the checkstay is used for fine-tuning mast bend and controlling mainsail shape. The result of having these loads on the runner and the checkstay properly adjusted is that you get the correct amount of support to keep the spar correctly curved and not pumping in a seaway.

Running backstays and top sailing performance are closely related, so it is worth taking some time to learn how the various systems work. It's a fact that the performance increase on boats with smaller mast sections and backstays is substantial when compared to boats with fatter and heavier spars. Therefore, knowing how to use runners properly should be a small price to pay for the big improvement in performance that you can get from your rig. Getting them properly adjusted takes only a few seconds once you know what to look for, and the results can be dramatic.

The Ubiquitous, Useful Boom Vang

Here's a cruising aid for trimming sails, preventing gybes, and improving performance

Rob MacLeod

I first became aware of the myth that cruising sailors aren't interested in performance when I bought my first boat. The salesman said to me, "If you're not going to race, you won't need a boom vang." That little piece of misinformation set my sailing back at least a year, if not two.

My boat handled well on an upwind course without a vang. But as I bore away to a reach and eased the sheet, the boom had more vertical movement than lateral. In short, as the sheet was eased, the boom would rise and destroy the trim at the leech as well as the shape of the sail – to say nothing of the sail's performance. The purpose of a boom vang is to keep the boom from rising when the mainsheet is eased. With a vang, there was nothing to maintain the downward tension on the boom off the wind.

To use a boom vang effectively, you must understand how the vang should be positioned and how to use and adjust it while under way. First, consider sail shape. Let's assume your sail has reasonable draft position and depth – roughly 40 to 50 percent aft of the luff and neither too deep nor too shallow. The question that remains is how much twist to have along the leech of the sail.

If you look up at the leech, you can see a line formed by the leech that runs from the boom to midway between the two top battens. The line will be fairly straight, with a slight curve to leeward. At the top of the sail, between the two top battens, the leech starts to curve gently back to wind-ward. This line indicates the amount of twist in the sail.

In general, the top batten should be parallel to the boom; you'll be able to see it if you lie flat on your back in the cockpit and look up at the edge of the top batten. The vang is what keeps the boom down and controls the amount of twist in the leech.

Although there are a number of excellent hydraulic and mechanical vang devices on the market, the standard boom vang is a block-and-tackle system that leads from a bale on the bottom of the boom to the base of the mast. The farther aft on the boom the vang is placed, the more effective it will be.

Imagine a boat with a 10-foot boom (for round numbers). A 20-pound weight suspended from the end of the boom will set the shape of the leech. To get the same downward effect from the center of the boom takes 40 pounds of weight. If the weight is placed one-quarter of the way along the boom from the mast, where most vangs are attached, the weight must be four times the original, or 80 pounds. In addition, as wind speed increases, pressure on the sail and equipment increases exponentially. In other words, as the wind speed doubles, the pressure on the sail increases four times. The need for sturdy vang equipment becomes readily apparent.

The boom vang provides the mechanical advantage to pull the boom down and keep it down. With a four-to-one purchase, or mechanical advantage, a crew member has to apply only 20 pounds of pressure to obtain an 80-pound pull on the boom to maintain the desired sail shape.

The lower attachment point of the vang should be as close as possible to the base of the mast. If the vang attaches to a padeye on the cabintop some distance aft of the mast base, as it does in some arrangements, when the mainsheet is eased out the vang pulls the boom not only forward and down, but also toward the centerline of the boat. This angle could interfere with quick mainsheet release.

Adjusting vang tension is no great mystery, even though some "racing-trainer" instructors I know tend to overemphasize the term "hard on the wind" when they describe setting up the twist of the main for sailing close-hauled. It's easy to read more into the phrase than is necessary; as a result, people often overtighten the vang, even in light winds or when they are sailing on a reach.

The vang is an extension of the mainsheet and should not be tensioned until after the mainsheet has been trimmed. The best time to set vang tension is while you are sailing upwind on a close-hauled course. Once you've got the appropriate sheet tension for the proper amount of twist, tighten the vang just enough to maintain that leech shape.

Off the wind – reaching and running – you may need to ease the vang off slightly to get a little more twist in the sail to depower it. If the vang control line is led aft to the cockpit through a jam cleat to a winch, these adjustments are easy to make, even for a shorthanded crew.

On a broad reach or run, you can releaf the boom vang tackle and use it as a preventer. Detach the end of the vang at the base of the mast and reattach it to the toerail or a padeye on the edge of the deck to keep the boom down and prevent the sail from gybing accidentally if the helmsman wanders off course. If the mainsail has toggles or slides on its foot with spaces in between, you can rig a preventer strap around the boom and attach the tackle to it; this arrangement spreads the load better over a section of the boom.

The vang has a number of non-sailing uses. For example, if a crew member should take an unscheduled swim and has to be retrieved from the water, trying to get that waterlogged person back into the boat can be like carrying a 200-pound bag full of jello up a sand dune. But you can make a crane by attaching the upper end of the vang to the outer end of the boom. Use the lower end to lift the person out of the water and swing him back aboard.

You can use a second vang to help keep shape in the genoa by using it as a barberhauler if the existing genoa track does not have sufficient fore-and-aft or lateral adjustment to set the sail properly. Attach one end of the vang to the clew of the genoa and lead the other to the toerail, handrail, or any place that improves the lead of the jibsheet and the shape of the foresail.

You can also use the vang to hoist an outboard from the dinghy onto the stern rail or, by attaching it to the end of the boom or a whisker pole, create a crane to drain a swamped dinghy or put the tender on deck.

Finally, remember that all vangs are not created equal. Racing sailboats tend to use vangs with greater mechanical advantage. These feature a metal support rod, or tube, that eliminates the need for a topping lift to hold the boom up. As the mainsail is lowered, the vang's metal tube structure keeps the boom from crashing to the deck. If you have a block-and-tackle vang, you also need a topping lift to keep the boom up.

The support tube system cannot be used as a preventer, however. In this case, you can tie a strong piece of line to the outboard end of the boom and lead it to a block forward of the shrouds. Secure the line, and you have a preventer that works very well against an accidental gybe.

Good performance is not just for the racing sailor. With any type of sailing, you can improve the performance of your mainsail by controlling the amount of twist in the leech with a strong and easily handled boom vang. If you don't have one, you're missing out on both speed and safety. That's what good sailing performance is all about.

Trimming the Cruising Mainsail

Here are some tips for making your boat seakindly over long hauls

Robert Hopkins, Jr.

───────────

Cruising sailors care as much about performance as any other sailor. The key to good cruising boat performance is balance. A boat's balance is determined by the way in which the sails interact with the keel and rudder. A well-balanced boat requires only a gentle, steady pull on the tiller to track in a straight line. If all else is equal, it is the leech of the mainsail that has the greatest effect in the shortest time on a boat's balance, and therefore its trim is critical.

The leech, of course, is the trailing edge of the main. In deflecting the air flowing off the sail, it determines the directional stability of the boat. If you consider your sails as the mirror image of your keel and rudder, the leech of the mainsail is, quite literally, your rudder in the air. It follows the sails overhead just as your rudder follows the keel underwater. The key here is to realize how inefficient it is for you to steer the boat using only one of your two rudders.

To take the simplest example, suppose you want to bear off from a beat to a reach. If you simply turn the rudder, the boat will bear off, but not without putting up a fight. To bear off more smoothly, the mainsail should be eased at the same time you turn the rudder so that the sails and underwater surfaces work in harmony. In heavy air many boats simply will not bear off until both the mainsail and the genoa are eased. A good many collisions are caused by neglecting to coordinate sail trim with steering changes.

The angle the mainsail leech presents to the wind is fundamental to upwind trim. A *closed*, or tight, leech deflects the airflow abruptly as it leaves the mainsail, which causes a large sideways force to develop to leeward at the boat's stern, which in turn pivots the bow to windward. A boat with this type of imbalance has *weather helm*; in order to counteract this force and continue steering in a straight line, the helmsman must angle the rudder as if to bear off. The more the leech is closed, the more weather helm it causes and the greater the rudder angle required to counteract it.

A little weather helm is advisable for many reasons. First, it makes the boat safer to sail. If you accidentally let go of the helm, the boat will swing up into the wind instead of bearing off into a gybe. Second, it helps your pointing ability by gently reminding you to head up as close to the wind as possible. Third, it has been proven that the rudder works most efficiently when it is angled slightly off centerline. And finally, a gentle pressure on the helm gives the boat *feel*, which keeps you in sensory touch with its performance. When old salts say they can sail upwind blindfolded, they mean that the boat has just enough weather helm to impart the feel they need to steer by the seat of their pants, or more specifically, by the touch of their fingertips.

Too much weather helm caused by too closed a leech makes the boat slow and fatiguing to sail. The helmsman fights the boat with his helm, exhausting himself because of the constant work required, particularly in heavy air. Underwater, the excessively angled rudder causes drag, while overhead the closed leech acts as a brake.

On the other hand, an *open*, or twisted, leech allows the air to flow easily off the mainsail without developing as much sideways force. The boat has less weather helm and in extreme cases even develops a lee helm in which the boat bears away if the helm is left untended. The open leech reduces drag to a minimum by eliminating the air-brake effect and by quelling the battle between the rudder and the leech. As a result, you tend to *foot* – sail low with less weather helm and fast with less drag. A boat with too open a leech might feel great to sail, but it does not point as high as it should. When it is trimmed correctly, the main should induce a moderate amount of weather helm through its moderately closed leech and cause a moderate but not detrimental amount of drag.

The correct trim procedure is a simple five-step process; here is how you would complete it on the water:

- Adjust twist with sheet tension until the top batten is parallel to the boom;

- Balance the boat with the traveler so that the rudder is angled between three degrees and eight degrees off the center;
- Set the depth of the mainsail with outhaul tension;
- Adjust draft position with luff tension until it is located 40 percent of the distance from the luff to the leech;
- Finally, evaluate the total power of the main and consider whether to reduce its power by reefing.

Upwind trim procedure begins by adjusting twist with the mainsheet tension until the top batten is parallel with the boom. Technically, twist is the change in the sheeting angles of the sail from bottom to top relative to the foot. Twist is what makes sail shape beautiful and complex. Twist matters to the performance of your boat.

To see how the mainsheet affects twist, stand directly under the midpoint of your boom and picture the chord lines at each batten height. Remain under the boom, play the mainsheet through a few inches, and observe what happens. If you ease the sheet, the boom rises up a lot and moves outboard slightly. As the boom rises, it allows the sail to twist. You can see twist increase by watching the upper chord line angles increases relative to the boom.

The best way to gauge twist from on board the boat is to observe the angle made between the top batten and the boom. In so doing, you aren't literally measuring twist, because the angle of the batten is different from the angle of the chord line, but the two are related.

The best average position for the top batten on every boat, from a dinghy to a 12-meter, is *parallel to the boom*. As you trim the sheet, the sail's twist lessens and the batten closes until it is parallel to the boom. Trimming harder takes away all the twist, closes the upper leech, and pokes the upper batten to windward. Easing the sheet produces the opposite result. From this you can see that trimming the sheet increases helm and easing it reduces helm. Sheet tension and traveler position are your two primary balance controls.

If you own a cruising mainsail without battens, your upper leech will be slightly rounder than usual because it lacks the stiffening support that an upper batten normally provides. This extra curvature will make your leech more closed where the batten ought to be. Therefore, an imaginary batten in that position will poke slightly to windward of the boom when the sail is correctly trimmed.

In light air, the weight of the boom might be enough to close the upper leech. In this case the batten will poke to windward without any sheet tension at all. In heavy air (over 20 knots true), you should ease the sheet slightly to open the top batten and spill air off the upper sail. Reducing power at the top of the rig helps keep the boat on her feet.

Now balance the boat with the traveler so that the rudder angle is between three and eight degrees. A smoothly working traveler makes a big difference to your upwind performance. The traveler is connected to your rudder in the wind, just as the tiller is connected to your rudder in the water. It controls the angle of the entire sail to the boat's centerline and to the wind. Trimming the traveler to windward closes the leech, which increases weather helm and the amount of rudder needed to steer in a straight line. An inch or two of traveler movement makes a big difference to the rudder angle.

Traveler trim also affects feel. But the problem with feel is that you can be fooled into feeling good when the boat is poorly balanced. To ensure you have everything truly balanced, you should actually *measure* the rudder angle, in degrees, off centerline, and then keep the angle between three and eight degrees.

In light air you may need to encourage weather helm by pulling the boom up to centerline (but not further) with the traveler. In medium air, most boats balance nicely, although if you want to be precise, play the traveler to give you a rudder angle of four to five degrees. In heavy air, the problem is keeping your helm angle under eight degrees by easing the traveler to leeward.

Now set the sail's depth with outhaul tension. Depth is the fullness of a sail expressed as a percent of its chord length. Since sails extract energy from the wind by changing its direction, and since a deep sail curves the wind more than a flat one does, the deep sail is more powerful.

Mainsail depth is determined mainly by the sail's design. It's up to your sailmaker to cut the sail so that it sets well on the mast, and it's up to you to adjust the outhaul so the sail looks relaxed. The outhaul lets you stretch the foot out to its intended tension for the breeze: tight for heavy air, eased for light air.

The tighter you pull on the outhaul, the flatter the lower third of the sail becomes. But a cruising sail is not as responsive to outhaul adjustments as a racing sail is. On a cruising sail, the outhaul is a *shape-maintaining* control, whereas on a racing sail with a foot shelf (an elliptically shaped panel of stretchy material, also called a lensfoot), it is a *shape-changing* control.

In light and medium air, set the outhaul so it barely removes the small vertical wrinkles rising from the boom into the sail. As the breeze freshens, more tension is required to eliminate the wrinkles caused by cloth stretch. In heavy air, tighten the outhaul until there are long horizontal creases running along the foot in the luffing sail. They will disappear when you fill the sail with wind. Always ease the mainsheet to reduce the forces on the sail before adjusting the outhaul.

Next adjust the sail's draft position, with luff tension, until the draft is 40 percent aft from the luff. Increasing luff tension moves the draft forward; easing it lets the draft back. However, the correct position for *every breeze* is 40 percent of the chord length aft from the luff. To maintain this shape as the breeze builds, stretching the cloth and bending the mast, you should increase luff tension. A good general rule is that the tension should be enough to eliminate any small horizontal wrinkles behind the mast.

Adjusting luff tension depends on how your mast is rigged. On rigs with a fixed boom, use the halyard itself, being sure to ease the mainsheet and the vang first. Other rigs allow you to hoist the halyard fully up and then adjust luff tension with a downhaul connected to a sliding boom. Another system (especially good for big boats with high loads) employs a fixed boom with a cunningham hole in the sail through which you pass a cunningham line to control luff tension. Whatever the system, the principle is the same. Use more tension in more breeze to keep the draft position 50 percent aft of the luff.

Finally, you must constantly evaluate the total power of the main and decide whether to reduce power by reefing. As the wind freshens, the boat heels and develops weather helm. You keep the helm angle under eight degrees primarily by lowering the traveler, but also by easing the sheet slightly to twist off the upper sections. You also increase the outhaul and luff tension as the cloth stretches. Eventually though, these remedies are not enough. Now you should throw in a reef to reduce the total sail area. Three factors affect your decision to reef.

First is your boat's natural limit of stability. It isn't designed to heel beyond a certain point without slowing down drastically. This maximum angle of heel, measured by a clinometer on racing boats, is typically 25 to 28 degrees. Old salts know the limit of stability as *rail down*, when the gunwale is nearly awash. Once your boat is rail down, it's time to reef.

Second is the mainsail's aerodynamic drag. As the wind increases, you should be easing the traveler to keep the rudder angle under eight degrees. As you ease, the main falls to leeward into the exhaust of the genoa, and it begins to backwind, forming a bubble in the luff. You can think of this type of backwind as unnecessary sail area that is being held in reserve for a lull. However, when more than half the sail is backwinded, your reserve is excessive. The bubble is causing too much drag, and now you should reef.

Finally there is prudence. When cruising shorthanded, exercise caution in heavy air and always reef on the early side. On a blustery day an experienced sailor throws in a reef at the mooring. If it's not needed, he or she has no trouble shaking it out once the boat is underway. This is far preferable to realizing how hard it's blowing only after you leave the harbor.

Trimming the main on the wind should not require all your conscious attention, not even half of it. A well-trimmed mainsail tends itself, and if it needs readjustment, it will tell you. Never ignore a tug on the helm – your two rudders are talking to each other.

The New Roller-Furling Headsail

On a short-handed cruise, there's no better friend than this sail

Wally Cross

━━━━━━━━━━

Good sailing products keep coming, and nowhere is this more evident than with today's roller-furling headsail systems and the wide range of furling genoas that are now available to the cruising sailor.

Not so long ago it took a crew of four to handle the big 150 percent genoa on a typical 30-footer. And a boat of this size probably had at least three different headsails to cover the full range of wind strengths; a 40-footer had four sails to accomplish the same thing. This arrangement was fine for racing skippers with organized crews, but the cruising sailor, not always blessed with an active and skilled crew, began to get tired of the amount of work needed to sail the boat efficiently.

Then the roller-furling system came into being. Popular acceptance was predictable, because roller furling makes the setting and stowing of the sail much easier. And you can leave a roller-furling headsail up all summer, making it easier than ever to simply run down to your boat and go for a sail.

The reasons that contemporary furling systems are so easy to operate are, first, the units have independent head and tack swivel systems; second, ball bearings are in every moving part; and third, the furling basket/drum at the bottom of the sail is large enough to work well under load.

In addition, the best sail systems allow the sail to be reefed, or partially furled, as well as completely furled – a situation that allows a sailmaker to design a single sail that can perform well in winds from 2 to 30 knots. These new "wide-range" genoas come out of a mixture of features that have produced a reefable sail that is strong enough to work in big winds yet light enough to remain properly shaped in the slow going.

What we see today is a "one-person" system, a combination of a roller-bearing furling unit and a radial-cut genoa that is constructed from new materials. This construction allows the sail to be reefed down to a smaller size. The combination allows the sail to give top performance over a wide range of wind conditions and still be easy to handle and provide excellent durability.

The key, of course, as with any good headsail, is to have it light, strong, and capable of holding its shape when it is reefed down. The best fabrics for this purpose seem to be a blend of Mylar and Dacron in a sandwich construction; they produce a light and flexible material.

The sail should be designed in a radial pattern that minimizes stretch and aligns the strongest Dacron material in the leech area, where the greatest loads occur. Using this material, sailmakers can build into these cruising genoas a "racing" shape to get even better performance for the cruising sailor.

In the past, roller-furling genoas tended to lose their designed draft as soon as the sail was being reefed. As the sail was rolled up, it would become very deep in the middle sections of the sail. The result would be, on a partially reefed sail, a very full draft sail that tended to make the boat heel over in higher winds and go more slowly.

These days, tape or foam that is placed along the luff of the sail keeps the sail flat, and the sail remains flat as it is rolled up. A flat profile helps the boat remain more upright, allowing it to sail faster. This upright configuration also helps the boat track through the water with less pressure on the helm.

Construction tips.   For your onboard reference, your sailmaker should stencil the foot of the sail at the theoretical tack points of the 135 percent, 110 percent, and 85 percent overlap. These points correspond to the reductions in sail area that you would experience if you actually changed conventional jibs, going down from the large 150 percent #1 headsail to a smaller 135 percent #2, and so forth.

New material with ultraviolet coating should also be part of every new roller-furling sail. In the past, roller-furling genoas had a second layer of material plied along the leech of the sail to combat the sun's damaging rays. The trouble was that this second layer of cloth usually distorted the shape of the sail, and the extra weight along the leech accelerated the breakdown of the basic material. The new coated materials not only protect the

APPARENT-WIND SPEED				
	0–15 knots	15–20 knots	20–25 knots	25–30 knots
Genoa overlap	150%	135%	110%	85%
Genoa lead	aft	forward 1'	forward 2'	forward 3'
Main hoist	full	full	full	reef
Maximum heel	5–15°	15–20°	15–20°	15–20°
Helm pressure	light	moderate	moderate	moderate
Trim off spreader	1 ft.	1.5 ft.	2 ft.	3 ft.
Leech and foot lines	light	moderate	mod.–heavy	heavy
Backstay pressure	light	moderate	heavy	heavy

Table 1 *Roller-furling genoa settings. This table shows typical settings at different apparent-wind speeds for a moderate-displacement 40-footer with a roller-furling headsail. The genoa-lead placement indicator assumes a clew height above the deck of 4 feet.*

sail, but also keep the weight down, and they work with a radial construction.

Other conveniences to consider include the addition of leech and foot cords to eliminate the fluttering of the sail in the wind. Slightly tensioning both the cords at the clew eliminates this flutter.

Finally, the clew of the sail should be cut high enough to minimize the need to move the jib leads any great distance when the sail is reefed down. This feature makes it possible to reef the sail quickly with just one person. Four feet above the deck on a 40-footer, three feet for a 30-footer, and so forth, is about right.

Sail trim. Generally speaking, the roller-furling headsail doesn't require any settings different from a conventional sail. There are, however, a few things you should keep in mind. Depending on the type of boat, the time to start reefing down is when the boat begins to experience either too much weather helm or too much heel. I feel 25 degrees of heel is about the maximum for any boat that is sailing to windward. When the boat starts to go beyond about 15 degrees, the apparent wind strength is at the point where you probably should reef the sail down to the 135 percent tack point.

If the apparent wind speed is approaching 20 knots, it is probably a good time to reef down to the 110 percent, or working jib, size. If the apparent wind gets over 25 knots, you next move is to reef down to the 85 percent, or "storm" jib, size. This is the point at which you probably want to start reefing the mainsail (although here again, depending on the boat type, it could be appropriate to reef the main a bit earlier).

Roller-furling headsails should never be trimmed in very tight against the shrouds; the full sail should never be closer than one foot from the end of the spreader. The same applies to the location of the trimming block. In almost all cases, a roller-furling headsail works best if it is trimmed slightly outboard of the point where a #1 genoa would be trimmed; on a 40-footer, the athwartships trim point for a roller-furling jib should be located about one foot farther outboard of the trimming point for a conventional jib.

The same "eased-trim" rule also applies to the mainsail. The reason is that if the headsail is trimmed a bit more outboard, the main can also be trimmed in a similar fashion and not be backwinded by the jib. The result is that the heeling forces will be less and the boat will not want to heel over or head up into the wind, which puts additional pressure on the helm. Even though the boat may not be pointing quite as high, it will be sailing on a more even keel and going faster.

The roller-furling jibsheets can be constructed of conventional Dacron, and each one should be tied to the clew of the sail with a bowline. However (and this is a point many people miss), when the sail is furled all the way up and is to be secured, make sure the sheets have two additional complete wraps around the rolled-up sail and the sheets are securely cleated, with just a slight tension. Taking those two extra wraps around the sail prevents any accidental unfurling of the jib if the wind starts to pick up when the boat is at a dock, on a mooring, or at anchor. Also make sure the line running to the furling drum is cleated securely so that it won't run out unexpectedly.

If you keep these design and trim ideas clearly in mind, you should have trouble-free sailing with these new roller-furling jibs. If you have a well-constructed furling system, you will find the sail is lighter, more useful, and more durable than ever before.

IV

Spinnaker Talk

The Cruising Spinnaker Exposed

*This sail is essential for
long-distance cruising*

Tim Yourieff

One of the most popular sails in the cruising sailor's inventory these days
is the asymmetrical, or cruising, spinnaker. It is known by a variety of
sailmaker trade names, such as Gennaker, Flasher, MPS, and Spanker. Unlike the conventional spinnaker, which is symmetrical on either side of its
centerline, the cruising spinnaker has a definite luff and leech, with the luff
being a bit longer than the leech. The sail is about 25 percent smaller in
total area than a standard spinnaker, but it is still about twice as large as a
150 percent genoa.

The cruising spinnaker is designed specifically to enhance a boat's
offwind performance. It will also make the sail safe and easy to handle
offwind - even when sailing shorthanded. Fulfilling this criterion leads to
another major difference between the cruising spinnaker and the conventional spinnaker.

The cruising spinnaker does not require a spinnaker pole because its
tack remains attached to the forestay no matter which tack the boat is on.
Gybing a standard spinnaker with a pole means moving the outboard pole
end from one clew to the other, and this is the moment when most spinna-
ker-handling problems occur. This is also what discourages many cruising
skippers from using the sail. They don't like to handle a conventional spinnaker with a pole unless they have a crew of experienced sailors on board.

The good thing about the cruising spinnaker is that you gybe that sail very much the same way you would if you were flying a genoa, thus avoiding the risk of an uncontrolled sail during the gybing maneuver.

There are two ways to hoist the sail. You can use either a spinnaker halyard or a genoa halyard, depending on the setup of your boat. There are, however, different attachment procedures and different sheet leads, depending on which halyard system you use.

Using the spinnaker halyard. My definition of a spinnaker halyard is one that exits the mast above the point where the headstay is attached. The halyard must also pass through a free-swiveling block, allowing it to pull from any direction without chafing.

To set the spinnaker using this halyard, first attach the halyard to the head ring on the sail. Do not use the snapshackle on the sail near the head (Fig. 1); rather, attach the snapshackle located near the tack directly to the headstay. If the genoa is furled on the forestay, however, you must snap on a set of parrel beads that have been wrapped around the furled sail (Fig. 2).

Parrel beads are solid nylon balls with holes drilled through them, through which a wire cable passes. The cable has stainless-steel thimbles at either end, and the snapshackle at the tack is attached to the thimbles to close the loop of beads around the sail. The parrel beads roll over the furled jib, allowing the tack of the cruising spinnaker to be raised and lowered with ease.

Next, tie the tack downhaul line to the tack ring, lead it through a turning block on the deck near the bow, and run it aft to a cleat or winch - preferably near the cockpit. Set up the tack downhaul so the tack of the sail is about five feet above the deck when the sail is hoisted.

Attach the spinnaker sheet to the clew ring of the spinnaker and make sure the line is led aft outside the lifelines to a turning block on the toerail located just forward of the stern pulpit. Then run it forward to a

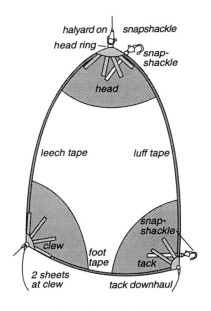

Fig. 1 *The cruising spinnaker is a versatile sail; it differs from a conventional spinnaker in that it has a definite luff and leech.*

winch. The sheet that is not being used - the lazy sheet - should also be led forward *in front of the headstay,* attached to the clew of the spinnaker, and then back on the other side of the boat - outside the shrouds and lifelines - to another turning block positioned just forward of the stern pulpit. Then take that sheet and lead it to a winch.

Now you are ready to hoist the sail. Start by heading off to a square run. Leave the mainsail fully out during the hoisting procedure. The mainsail will blanket the spinnaker and keep it from filling until you are ready for it to be set. A good place to raise the sail is from the leeward side, just ahead of the boom.

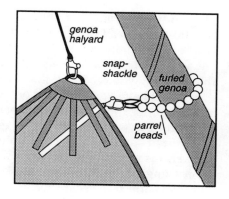

Fig. 2 *Using parrel beads with either a genoa or a spinnaker halyard allows you to hoist a cruising spinnaker even if the genoa is furled on the headstay. The snapshackle at the head should be used only with a genoa halyard.*

Once it is fully hoisted, slowly head up to your desired course and pull in the sheet until the sail sets. Make sure you have three turns of the sheet around the winch. Now you are sailing with your cruising spinnaker.

Gybing the sail. Ease out the spinnaker sheet until the sail collapses in front of the headstay. Don't lose the end of the sheet. Then bear away to a dead run and pull the mainsail to the centerline. To complete the gybe, ease out the mainsail on the new gybe, and head up onto your new course. Pull in the new spinnaker sheet (the lazy sheet on the previous tack) until the sail is pulled completely around the front of the headstay and is set correctly for the new course. This completes your gybe.

Lowering the sail. Bear away onto a dead run, but this time keep the mainsail eased out. Do not ease the spinnaker sheet. The sail will collapse once the mainsail blankets it. Have one person ease the halyard while another pulls the sail down by pulling on the leech. Ideally, whoever is pulling the sail in should be positioned on the leeward side of the boat just in front of the boom. This position will insure that the spinnaker remains blanketed by the mainsail until it is completely lowered to the deck.

Using the genoa halyard. A genoa halyard exits the mast through a sheave *below* the point where the headstay is attached. The halyard is restricted in its motion and must pull in an essentially forward direction to avoid being chafed by the edge of the sheave box.

To set the spinnaker with a halyard configuration, attach the genoa halyard to the head ring on the sail. Then attach the snapshackle near the head of the sail directly to the headstay. This keeps the head of the sail in line with the front of the halyard sheave box and thereby avoids halyard chafe, which would occur if the sail were allowed to pull off to leeward.

If you have a genoa furled on the headstay, however, the snapshackle must first be snapped onto a set of parrel beads. Make sure the genoa sheets are running down along the furled genoa from the genoa clew, because the parrel beads at the head of the spinnaker must be able to go over both these sheets and over the furled sail in order to get them past the clew as the cruising spinnaker is hoisted.

Next attach the snapshackle near the tack of the spinnaker either to the forestay or to a second set of parrel beads if there is a roller-furling genoa on the stay. Set up the tack downhaul in the same way described earlier.

Now tie the sheet being used to the clew ring of the sail and lead it outside the lifelines aft to the turning block on the toerail and then to a winch. The lazy sheet should also be tied to the clew and led forward outside the shrouds. But this time lead it in front of the mast and *not* in front of the forestay, which is what you do with a spinnaker-halyard arrangement. Lead the lazy sheet aft on the other side of the boat, outside the shrouds and lifelines to the turning block, and then forward to the winch.

To hoist the cruising spinnaker with the genoa halyard, the procedure is exactly the same as it is with the spinnaker halyard. Head off, blanket the spinnaker with the mainsail, and hoist the spinnaker in the lee of the main.

To gybe the sail, first bear away to a dead run. Leave the mainsail eased out. The main will blanket the spinnaker and cause it to collapse.

Pull in the lazy sheet after you have made sure you have at least two turns on the winch. At the same time, ease out on the old sheet. With this procedure you are pulling the sail through the space between the headstay and the mast. This is different from having the sail clew go in front of the forestay during the gybe, which is what happens when you use the spinnaker-halyard method.

Bring the mainsail to the centerline, then complete the gybe and head up to your new course, trimming the sails as you come closer to the wind. To lower the spinnaker with the genoa halyard, proceed in exactly the same way that you would with a spinnaker halyard.

Basic cruising spinnaker trim.   There are two basic adjustments that you can make. The first deals with the height of the tack above the deck, and the second is the amount of sheet you should pull in for any given point of sail.

As a general rule, on a close reach the tack should be pulled down so the luff of the sail is nearly straight. On a very broad reach or run, the tack should be eased off considerably - approximately three feet on a 35-foot boat. On this point of sail you should get the tack as high as possible, but not so high that the sail starts to oscillate. This makes the sail, and the boat, unstable. On a beam reach, the tack height should be adjusted so it is somewhere between the high and the low positions.

A cruising spinnaker should be trimmed just enough to stop the luff from curling. Adjust the tack height so the middle of the luff curls first when you head the boat up. If the upper part of the luff curls first, the tack is too high and must be lowered. Conversely, if the lower part of the luff starts to curl first, the tack is too low.

Finally, a few words about the merits of the dousing sock. Though there are any number of trade names - "chute scoops," "stashers," "spanker socks" - the purpose of all these items is the same: They contain the spinnaker in a "sausage" bag during the hoisting and lowering process.

When you hoist the spinnaker, it is inside the sock and therefore will not fill unless you raise the sock to the top of the spinnaker. To make the sail collapse, pull the sock down over the spinnaker. This spills the wind out of the sail and makes it very easy to control while you are lowering it to the deck.

My recommendation is to use a sock if your boat is over 30 feet. The control lines are easy to handle, and having the spinnaker inside the sausage when you lower it to the deck makes it easy to put the whole rig into a sailbag. Once it is there, you know it is ready for the next time you want to go faster downwind, which is just the time you want to use your cruising spinnaker.

Get Your Spinnaker Flying Right

Here are some professional secrets for better performance

Tom Whidden

Let's take a good look at the spinnaker. First, it is typically bigger than other sails. At 180 percent overlap, it is significantly bigger than either a mainsail or jib. It has no control devices running the length of any of its sides; rather, it has two fixed points: the halyard at the top and the end of the pole at the bottom. A spinnaker is not much different from other sails, and there are four things you can do to affect its shape:

- Raise and lower the pole to change the sail's depth, particularly at the top.
- Raise and lower the pole to change where the depth, or draft, falls.
- Trim the pole back and forth to change the sail's angle of attack.
- Change the spinnaker-sheet lead to control power as well as the depth of the sail at the bottom.

Amount of draft. The basic rule of thumb is that the closer the leeches are to each other, the deeper the sail. When you lower the outboard end of the pole, the two leeches get tighter, they move closer together, and the sail becomes deeper. This, by the way, runs contrary to popular wisdom. In contrast, when you raise the pole, the leeches move farther apart and the sail gets flatter (Fig. 1).

Pole height, in addition to controlling depth, affects where the draft falls. Think of pole height as a cunningham in a mainsail. When you lower the pole (tighten the cunningham), the draft moves forward. Raise the pole (loosen the cunningham), and draft moves aft.

When we discuss draft, we are really talking about the shape of the sail's leading edge, or luff. As with a jib, an even break along the luff is most desirable in a spinnaker. Where the draft falls, which is a function of pole height, determines whether the sail luffs evenly or not.

Pole height is critical to proper spinnaker trim and should be adjusted as conditions warrant. The important thing is to have just the right amount of luff curve. Having the pole too low puts too much fullness in the luff, stalling it in that area. If the pole is too high, the luff becomes unstable and the sail will need to be overtrimmed to keep it from collapsing.

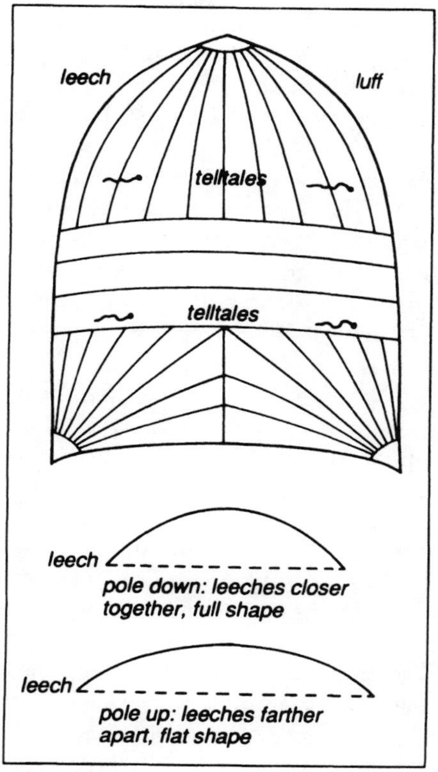

Illustrations by Kathy Bray

Fig. 1 *Telltales are helpful in determining pole height on a reach. If the pole is too high, the bottom telltale flutters first. If the pole is too low, the top telltale will flutter first.*

Correct pole position is desirable while you are running, but it is critical while reaching, particularly with a specialty reaching chute. Here the general rule is the flatter the sail, the lower the pole. On a reach, where the airflow is still attached, telltales on the spinnaker can indicate proper pole height. Both the top and bottom telltales should act the same. If not, raise or lower the pole accordingly.

If the pole is too high when reaching, the bottom telltale flutters first, and the sail breaks at the bottom first. If the pole is too low, the top telltale flutters first and the break starts at the top. Telltales not only provide an early warning of improper sail trim, but also are a better trim device than easing the sail until there is a curl in the luff. Easing the spinnaker out to the curl (the traditional method) actually reduces sail area.

Telltales aren't much help when you are running, because the flow is stalled. So here you can ease the sail until the luff curls, but don't overdo it, because a curl does diminish area. Your goal is still to have the spinnaker luff, or break, evenly up and down its leading edge. Remember, if the pole is too high, the lower luff curls before the upper. If the pole is too low, the upper luff curls first.

Angle of attack.   When the apparent wind is aft of 120 degrees, the pole should generally be squared, or at right angles, to the wind. This right-angle rule produces maximum separation between the spinnaker and the mainsail, which is desirable. With the apparent wind forward of 120 degrees, the pole should be over-squared, or less than 90 degrees to the wind (Fig. 2). Over-squaring the pole keeps the spinnaker from getting too full and thus too inefficient to be fast on a reach.

Over- or under-squaring the pole also affects draft. When the pole is over-squared, the sheet requires more tension to keep the sail full, making the foot of the sail flatter. When the pole is under-squared, the sheet can be eased further, making the sail fuller.

Generally, the inboard end of the pole should be at the same height as the outboard end, thus keeping the spinnaker as far from the mainsail as possible. This separation means the mainsail doesn't have to be over-trimmed, which contributes to excessive heel.

Because of its light weight and large size, the spinnaker is the most important sail on a reach or run; therefore, never sacrifice spinnaker trim for mainsail trim. If trim on one has to be sacrificed, let it be the mainsail.

The spinnaker sheet.   The spinnaker sheet is analogous to the genoa sheet and controls angle of attack. The sheet also controls power in the sail by controlling leech twist. Many sailors run the spinnaker sheet to the back of the boat and forget about it. In fact, the sheet lead should be determined by wind angle and wind speed. The theme of this exercise is always to maximize the sail's power without overwhelming the boat's stability. Even when it's reaching, a boat shouldn't heel much beyond 25 or 28 degrees.

When you are reaching in light air, move the sheet lead forward to minimize twist and add power. In medium air, move the lead back to free the leech and keep the airflow from stalling. In heavy air, run the sheet to the back of the boat to keep the powerful bottom sections of the spinnaker flat and the upper leech area open and twisted.

Running in light air, have the sheet lead located just under the boom. This tightens the leech and gives the sail more curvature - and therefore more stability. The only time you might want to move the lead forward of that position is if the wind is light but seas are erratic.

When you are running in medium air, keep the lead in the same place as in light air. This allows the sail to lift as high as it can without having the leech twisting off.

When you are running in heavy air, make sure the sheet lead is led farther forward of the boom. This prevents chafe on the sheet and keeps the spinnaker from oscillating, which helps keep the boat under control.

An alternative to moving the spinnaker lead is using a barberhauler, which typically is a line running through a block that is attached anywhere on the rail. With this system, the sheet lead can be left at the back of the boat. Then the lead angle can be

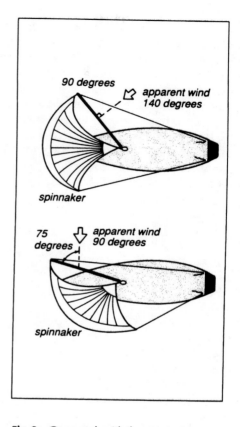

Fig. 2 *On a reach with the apparent wind greater than 120 degrees, set the pole square to the apparent-wind angle. At less than 120 degrees, set the pole so it is less than 90 degrees; 75 degrees is a good approximation.*

changed by moving the barberhauler. Because it is far easier to move the barberhauler than the sheet lead, you can experiment with the lead position and pin down the optimum lead positions for your boat.

The staysail. The staysail works best when the wind is 75 to 120 degrees apparent and moderate to fresh and the water is fairly smooth. Even then, numbers aren't carved in stone - a more important number is that which is on the boat's knotmeter. Check your boat's speed a minute before you hoist the staysail and two minutes after. If it doesn't appear to be working well and speed doesn't increase, take it down.

Generally, when apparent wind is on the beam or forward of it, tack the staysail on centerline. When you free up and the spinnaker pole comes aft, the tack can be moved to the weather side. In ideal conditions (close reach, fresh air, smooth water), the staysail can be tacked well forward. In lighter wind, tack it aft to give the spinnaker more breathing room.

A staysail's effect on the spinnaker is often so direct that when the spinnaker collapses, the staysail has to be luffed or even dropped entirely before the spinnaker refills. If this collapsing happens regularly, the smartest thing to do is take the staysail down.

How to Catch a "Tow" Downwind

It's a tough technique to master, but a pleasure to use

Ed Baird

———————

At seminars I give on racing techniques, I am always asked about how a sailboat "tows" another boat downwind. Does the leading boat slow down when a trailing boat rides on its wake? How much does it help the boat astern? Where is the best place to be to catch a wake?

The fact is that catching a tow, or drafting, off a faster boat can give you big gains. The potential is so great that positioning yourself for a tow should be an important part of your strategy whenever you round a windward mark ahead of a larger or a faster boat.

But getting into a spot where you can catch a tow is tricky. Knowing how and when to try, and how to work with the towing boat, can mean the difference between big gains and a big disappointment.

The gains.   Suppose your boat's hull speed on a spinnaker reach is 6.35 knots in 12 knots of true wind. Along comes a slightly larger boat with a hull speed of 6.55 knots. The seas are relatively smooth, and you have a long way to go to the next mark. The other boat goes by you, you hop a tow, and your top speed immediately jumps to 6.55 knots.

As long as you stay on the tow, you're going 0.2 knot faster than you should be able to under your own sail power. That's free speed. If you get a tow for half an hour, you gain 0.1 mile on your competition; two hours gets you a 0.4 mile gain. If you can remain on a tow behind a boat going 0.4 knot faster, you gain twice as much.

Stock Newport/Onne Van Der Wal

Photo 1   *Catching a tow in light air is almost impossible, but as the wind builds, the opportunities improve. Sea condition is another important factor.*

How it works.   As a boat moves through the water, it digs a hole in the water creating a bow wave and a stern wave. The distance between the two wave crests is basically the waterline length of the boat. Although these waves move diagonally relative to the centerline of the boat, there is also a wave astern that runs perpendicular to the boat's course and also moves at the same speed as the boat.

Because the stern wave moves at the same speed as the boat, this is the wave to use when you want to be towed by a faster boat. The action is similar to the drafting technique used by race-car drivers and bicycle racers who want to go faster without increasing power.

Any boat directly astern of another boat is sailing in water that is moving in the same direction. Therefore, the boat astern will move over the bottom faster (assuming the boat ahead is faster) than it would if it were sailing in water that is undisturbed by a wake (Fig. 1).

So much for the theory; let's see how you can jump on a tow and use it to your advantage. Towing works for a boat of any size that is not sailing in a planing condition. Once on my Laser, I hooked a great tow when a Thistle went by on a light-air reach. The Thistle was creating enough

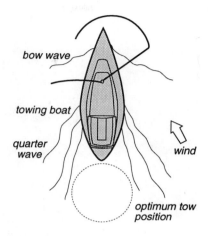

Fig. 1 *The water inside the dashed circle is being dragged along by the tow boat, and that means less resistance (because the water is moving forward) for the boat positioned directly behind the tow boat.*

wake for me to ride on it, and by the time we got to the gybe mark, the rest of the Laser fleet was hundreds of yards astern.

However, you don't need to be sailing on boats of different sizes as long as one boat is moving faster than the other. Racing in J/24s, I once sailed up to the leading boat as we were reaching along, and he waved us by. We went past him, he hopped a tow astern, and both of us sailed away from the rest of the fleet. Ashore after the race he told me he knew we were fast off the wind, so he used us to help him pull away from the other boats.

Hooking up. Conditions have to be right for towing, so look at the accompanying table to learn what conditions are best for catching a tow. Practice the maneuver in easy conditions like a stable, powerful jib reach. Then move on to more difficult conditions, such as choppy water or a close spinnaker reach. Your tactician or navigator should be the one who alerts the crew to what the towing conditions are before every offwind leg.

The way to catch a tow is to position yourself directly in front of a faster boat as it approaches you. Try to choose a boat that is sailing 0.1 or 0.2 knot faster than you are; a greater speed difference will make it hard for you to keep up with the lead boat.

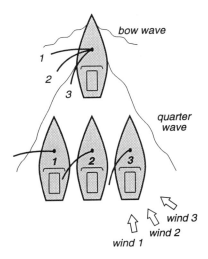

bow wave

quarter
wave

wind 3
wind 2
wind 1

Fig. 2   *The best spot to get a tow and keep the boat ahead from getting upset depends on wind angle: (1) running, give the boat ahead clear air; (2) reaching, follow the path of least resistance, which is directly astern; (3) close reaching, keep your air clear.*

When the overtaking boat gets close, a confident wave or a call saying "go ahead" is enough to keep your opponents from worrying about your intentions and possibly sailing high of their course.

As they sail by you to windward, you should try to keep about a boat's length of water between the two boats. When the other boat has moved ahead enough that you can head up and clear its stern, do so. Refill your chute if bad air has collapsed it, retrim the jib and main, and level out right behind the other boat. If you do it right, your bow should be just a few feet behind its transom. Now you're locked in on the wave, and you can ride as long as there's a wake and wind.

Most of the time it's best to be directly astern of the boat ahead because that is where the wake is largest. On a tight jib reach, working the upwind side of the wake helps keep your air clear. On a dead run, staying on the downwind side of the wake keeps the lead boat's air clear so you both can sail faster (Fig. 2).

Staying there.   In smooth water it's easy to stay right astern of a towing boat. Sometimes in rough water and windy conditions, you may catch both the leading boat's wave and a normal wave at the same time. When that happens, you could ride right up on the other boat. The key to avoiding a foul (the overtaking boat must give way) but still maintaining the tow is to know where to go if you get into this situation.

Remember that the boat ahead of you is your friend - it's not someone you're trying to pass. However, also keep in mind that you are a nuisance to it, so don't threaten the crew ahead or invite retaliation by overlapping to windward. If you do, they will probably luff you up to protect their air. If it's windy, you could broach and lose your tow position. At the very least, you both could sail high of the course and lose valuable distance to the mark.

Diving to leeward keeps the other boat visible, keeps it as the windward boat if you do establish an overlap, and keeps the other crew from feeling that you are trying to pass them. Remember that the boat ahead of you is faster (that's why it's there), and when the wave has gone by, it will be towing you again. Diving down to leeward also reduces your chances of broaching, since you have to ease the sails to depower.

Does towing hurt?   The towing boat does get hurt slightly, in two ways. First, its position relative to the boat immediately astern doesn't improve. However, since the towing boat isn't going slower, it's not losing against the rest of the fleet.

Second, any boat sailing very close astern can be a distraction. There is nothing more annoying than starting a long reaching leg with a boat right on your transom. However, the truth is that if a boat is on your transom, it is almost impossible to shake it, and worrying about it is only going to slow you down.

It's hard for the lead boat to shake free, but there are a couple of ways. The best way is to slow down until there isn't enough wake for the boat astern to ride. Sailing low in the light spots can slow the boat drastically. The trailing boat, which must follow to stay on the ride, falls astern as the wake drops. Note that if you are the lead boat, you are not violating Racing Rule 39 by sailing below a proper course because the trailing boat is not steering a course that is to leeward of the lead boat.

A second way to shake a boat astern is to head up until either the chute on the boat astern collapses or the boat broaches. This technique might backfire, of course, because the lead boat might broach first. What usually

		Apparent-wind direction (degrees)							
		<50		50–90		90–150		150–180	
True-wind speed (knots)		waves	smooth water	waves	smooth water	waves	smooth water	waves	smooth water
	0–6	no	no	no	no	no	no	no	no
	6–10	no	maybe	maybe	maybe	no	maybe	no	no
	10–15	maybe	yes	yes	yes	yes	yes	maybe	maybe
	15+	yes	yes	yes	yes	yes	yes	yes	yes

Table 1   *When are conditions right for towing?*

happens then is that the towed boat sails straight ahead, waits for the leader to catch up, and then jumps on the tow again. But even if this move does work, it involves sailing well above the best course to the next mark. Losing the fleet for the sake of one boat is never smart.

If you are the towing boat, your best defense is to mount a good offense. If you see a smaller boat ahead of you and you think it is going to try to catch a tow, give it a wide berth as you go by. If it can't get on that first wave, catching a tow gets harder and harder as it falls astern.

Towing can produce big gains when it's used in the right conditions. So any time you're sailing off the wind and the conditions are favorable, move yourself over to a position that will allow you to catch a ride on a passing boat's wake. Doing so will be more valuable than fighting it out for position with the one or two boats that are sailing along next to you at the same speed.

Is Your Spinnaker Big Enough?

*If you race under IMS,
your sail may be too small*

John Collins

If you are serious about racing, you should have the maximum amount of anything that adds speed to your boat, particularly your sails. They should be the largest the rules allow. Yet when it comes to ocean racing, much of the nomenclature and measurement traditions come from the old Cruising Club of America rating rule, which was replaced by the International Off-shore Rule in 1970. The CCA and the IOR rule still affect spinnaker size for contemporary racers.

Under both rules the length of the spinnaker luff is limited by the following formula: SL(spinnaker length) $= 0.95\, I + JC$, where I is the height of the foretriangle and JC is the corrected length of the base of the foretriangle. The JC length is the largest of the following three measurements: the distance from the front of the mast at the deck to the intersection of the headstay and the sheer; the length of the spinnaker pole (SPL); or the maximum spinnaker width (SMW) divided by 1.8 (Fig. 1).

I is the larger of the following two numbers: the measurement from the intersection point of the headstay and either the forward side of the mast corrected for the presence of a crane (a forestay outrigger under the IOR) or the underside of the spinnaker halyard when drawn horizontally from the mast to the level of the sheer line when abreast of the mast. A corrected factor of four percent of the rated beam (B) is intended to simulate the crown of the deck.

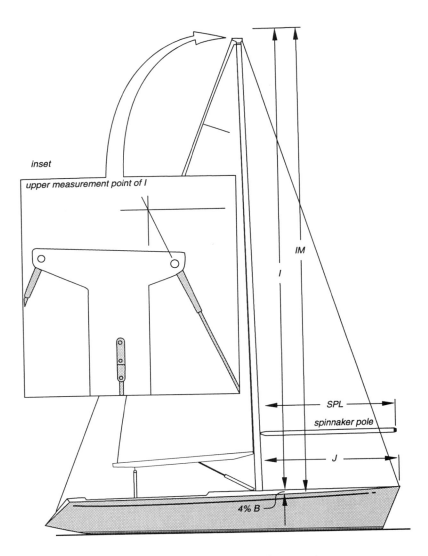

Fig. 1 *Although standard measurement points are the same, the new computation is different. The difference between the old I measurement and the new IM measurement is that a correction of 4 percent of rated beam is no longer present; that means the spinnaker can be several inches longer than under the old measurement.*

That *I* measurement is defined as being on the centerline of the boat. This is the definition most designers use when they draw out a sailplan. However, the International Measurement System (IMS) rule has changed all this. The IMS has eliminated the deck crown correction of four percent and uses instead the foretriangle height, designated *IM*, to determine the maximum spinnaker luff/leech length permitted. This means it is going to be several inches longer than the old *I*.

Because the rated beam of a modern 40-foot ocean racer will be in the 12- to 13-foot range, the difference between the old IOR *I* and the new IMS *IM* will be on the order of about a half a foot. This represents about a one percent increase in the size of the IMS spinnaker.

Spinnaker's too small. In looking over a number of certificates for new boats built to the IMS rule, I noticed most have spinnaker luff/leech lengths that are under the maximum length allowed by the IMS rule, some by as much as four percent of *B*. I concluded that sails are being built using the old definition of *I* instead of the new *IM*.

I should add that I don't believe the undersized luff/leech lengths are a "stretch" allowance, primarily because spinnaker materials tend to shrink with age. The shrinkage factor is big enough that some sailmakers regularly build a one-design spinnaker slightly oversized and then tell the customer to use the sail a few times before getting it measured.

The IMS Velocity Prediction Program (VPP) used to score races *always* assumes that a spinnaker is the maximum size permitted by the boat's rig dimensions. Conversely, it gives no credit for a spinnaker that is undersized. Therefore, if your spinnaker is undersized, you are throwing away time.

How much boat speed does an undersized spinnaker cost you? To find out, I used my old favorite, the computerized (PC compatible) version of the VPP, available from U.S. Sailing, P.O. Box 209, Newport, RI 02840. This VPP assumes that a spinnaker is as large as the rules allow, but the latest version has an option that lets you ignore the IMS and produce speed estimates based on the actual sail size. This makes it easy to see what effect a smaller spinnaker has on the predicted boat speed.

True, the predicted speed loss for a 40-footer is not dramatic. But it could be the difference in a close race. For a 40-foot ocean racer flying a spinnaker six inches short of the IMS-allowed maximum, the predicted speed loss is about 0.01 knot in six knots of wind, at the optimum downwind sailing angle. The speed-loss difference decreases with increasing wind speed. In 12 knots of wind, the loss is 0.007 knot, and in 20 knots the loss is 0.006 knot.

Although this is not a level of detail you are apt to notice on your knotmeter, if you look at the speed loss in terms of ratings for various wind mixes on the IMS certificate, it's a different story. In a six-knot wind, it amounts to a loss of one second per mile on a windward/leeward course. And at 12 knots, the loss is 0.4 second per mile. Obviously the loss is smaller with other race course patterns because there is less downwind sailing.

Look at it this way: How would you like to have had another 10 or 20 seconds in that last close race? And don't forget, these seconds are free. At least, they are "free" until your sailmaker figures out he or she should be charging a bit more for a spinnaker built to the new rule.

Getting Max Speed from Asymmetrical Sails

Racing with a cruising sailor's old standby requires new knowledge

Wally Cross

———————————

In the world of performance sailing, there's a lot of talk about asymmetrical spinnakers. The idea isn't really new, of course; cruising sailors have been using asymmetrical spinnakers without a spinnaker pole since the early 1970s.

These sails continue to be improved, and if they receive wider acceptance among racing fleets, racing sailors could reap big benefits, because a two-spinnaker sail inventory will be possible. There will be an asymmetrical sail for reaching and a symmetrical spinnaker for downwind.

Cruising spinnakers. Cruising spinnakers are about 15 percent narrower than traditional spinnakers, which makes them pretty easy to set and fly without a spinnaker pole. In a typical cruising setup, the asymmetrical's tack is attached to a rope pennant that can be raised or lowered to match the wind strength and direction.

When the wind is slightly forward of the beam, the tack of a cruising asymmetrical should be set reasonably close to deck level; in this position the sail looks and performs much like a genoa. When the wind is aft of the beam, the tack pennant should be eased to make the luff fuller. In this configuration the sail becomes more like a conventional spinnaker. When a snuffer, or sock, is pulled down over the sail to keep it from filling, one or two people can raise and lower the sail with ease.

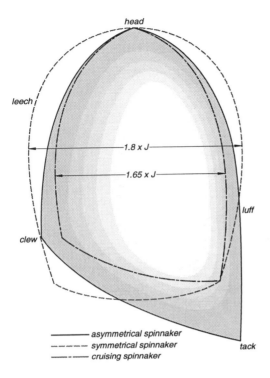

asymmetrical spinnaker
symmetrical spinnaker
cruising spinnaker

Fig. 1 *Cruising, symmetrical, and asymmetrical spinnakers vary in width and in luff length.*

Asymmetrical chutes for racing. The traditional symmetrical spinnaker has luffs of equal length; it is the sail most racers use whenever the apparent-wind angle is greater than about 60 degrees. However, the new performance-oriented asymmetrical spinnakers, flown from a pole, are as wide as symmetrical chutes, about $1.8 \times J$ (the base of the foretriangle from the mast to the headstay), but the luff of the sail is about 20 percent longer than the leech (Fig. 1). This type of sail is becoming very popular in some one-design classes. It is also available on the latest models from J Boats (whose designs feature an extendible bow pole or sprit) and are acceptable in a number of PHRF fleets.

These new asymmetricals are very different from both cruising spinnakers and traditional symmetrical spinnakers. They can be made from a variety of materials, including Kevlar, polyester, and a number of different nylons. They can be very fast off the wind, and ongoing sail development programs will raise the crossover point, the wind speed at which a symmetrical spinnaker is faster than an asymmetrical.

Currently, asymmetricals are very fast for reaching when the true wind is 10 knots or less and forward of the beam. The sail's long luff and generous width make it very stable and give it a far better shape for these conditions than the symmetrical.

To increase the effective range of these asymmetrical spinnakers, some PHRF fleets are allowing the spinnaker pole to be moved aft, off the centerline and away from the headstay. As a result, it should be possible to sail even deeper angles (headings on which the apparent wind is farther aft) with asymmetricals.

Handling the new asymmetricals. When you rig an asymmetrical, if the spinnaker halyard block is above the headstay, you must lead the sheets so both of them run outside the headstay. If the halyard block is at the same height or lower than the headstay, lead the spinnaker sheets inside the stay.

An asymmetrical should be trimmed as you would a conventional spinnaker, with a few additional elements of genoa trim. First, you should always ease the sheet enough that there is some curl in the luff, and you should keep the pole as low as possible. On most boats the sheet lead runs aft to the stern quarter.

Just as with a genoa, the best way to determine the optimum sheet angle for an asymmetrical is to put three sets of telltales on the leading edge of the sail about 18 inches back from the luff. The sheet lead should be adjusted the way it is for a jib. If the top telltales luff first, move the sheet lead forward. If the bottom set luffs first, move the lead aft. The objective is to have all three sets break together (Fig. 2).

Gybing an asymmetrical spinnaker with a pole is a little different from gybing a symmetrical one. Since the asymmetrical spinnaker's tack must remain at the bow while the pole is moved from one side of the headstay to the other, the clew should always have two sheets attached to it, and you need a tack pennant at the bow to which you can attach the tack of the sail while moving the pole to the windward side of the headstay. This pennant should be strong and fitted with a quick-release shackle (Fig. 3).

To lower an asymmetrical without using a snuffer, first raise the jib inside the asymmetrical and

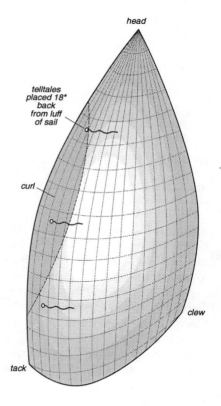

Fig. 2 *When an asymmetrical is trimmed properly, the luff of the sail should curl, but the three sets of telltales should also break together.*

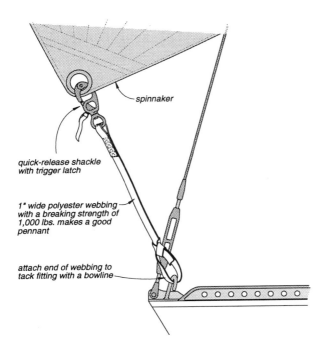

spinnaker

quick-release shackle
with trigger latch

1" wide polyester webbing
with a breaking strength of
1,000 lbs. makes a good
pennant

attach end of webbing to
tack fitting with a bowline

Fig. 3   *A good tack pennant consists of a 3-foot length of polyester webbing and a quick-release shackle with a trigger latch.*

get it pulling. Then have a crew member grasp the asymmetrical's weather sheet and stand on the foredeck to windward about midway between the tack and the clew of the jib. When it is time to lower the asymmetrical, lower the halyard slowly while the person to windward of the jib pulls the windward sheet and brings the sail down to the deck to leeward of the jib. The sail's afterguy should also be released as the sail is being lowered. Once the sail is all the way down, put it down the forward hatch or take it aft and put it below for packing.

If you know how to trim an asymmetrical properly, and you can use it in your fleet, there's little question that it will be noticeably faster than a conventional spinnaker in apparent winds of less than 90 degrees. Once you get above 90 degrees, its effectiveness will vary from boat to boat, depending mainly on displacement. Even so, there is no denying that the new asymmetrical sails are exciting, and they are a good choice for any sailor interested in improved offwind performance.

Designing a Proper Spinnaker

Give a big sail a little respect and it will be easier to handle

Sally Lindsay

━━━━━━━━━━

When I was six years old the spinnaker was the scariest thing in the boat. At hoists, gybes and douses all of us "little kids" were ordered below. We would press against the ports to watch, our hearts pounding, until the shouting, crashing, rolling, and winch-grinding were over. Then we would re-emerge, saucer-eyed and subdued. As I grew, the little-girl fear was replaced by fascination. But the respect continued to grow. When I started sailing dinghies, the spinnaker still was the most enigmatic and challenging of the sails to handle. When I became a sailmaker, it became the most interesting sail to design and build.

The design and construction of spinnakers can be completely separated from that of a main or jib. Cloth stretch and broadseam amounts are on a different order of magnitude. Seaming, finishing, and testing are entirely different even though there are many theoretical parallels. Flow data from main and jib research can be applied to modern spinnaker design.

In the past, spinnakers were too full to permit an attached flow from luff to leech. The air separated and became turbulent, creating a constantly stalled foil which worked only because it presented sufficient projected area to push the boat downwind. On modern high-performance boats, spinnakers should encourage attached air flow across the major part of the sail, similar to the flow from luff to leech on upwind sails. But to take advantage of this, spinnakers must be much flatter than what was thought possible in the past.

In early spinnaker design there was no alternative to a full sail. Cloth stretch turned any sail into a baggy, tight-leeched sack, and there was no possibility of experimenting with flatter sails. Then, a Marblehead sailmaker, Bruce Dyson, realized that his Tempest would go faster with a flatter chute. This high-performance Olympic keelboat had more sail than two normal-sized people could effectively handle in a blow, and flattening the sails made her easier to handle. Dyson used two-ounce Dacron sailcloth in his spinnaker. It did not stretch, and for several years his chutes were the choice in heavy air. Then came Dynac - a regular nylon spinnaker cloth (half-ounce, three-quarter-ounce, or 1.6-ounce) that has been coated to greatly reduce stretch.

Now that it is possible to build spinnakers with more controlled cloth it is becoming apparent that flatter sails supply all the required lift (the force that makes you go forward), without as much drag (the force that slows you down). Fuller sails provide more "power," but they also heel the boat, load the centerboard to the point of stalling (which drives the boat sideways), and stall the whole sail plan by choking the slot with their tight leeches (Fig. 1). The idea is to keep the lift/drag ratio as efficient as possible: maximize the lift while minimizing the drag. This ratio varies with the particular characteristics and requirements of each class.

The overall depth of the sail is important, and so is its shape. Both the horizontal and vertical curves must be considered. The horizontal curves are called chords, the vertical curves are mitres (Fig. 2). A spinnaker may have chords that are full at the leeches and flat in the center like a Frisbee;

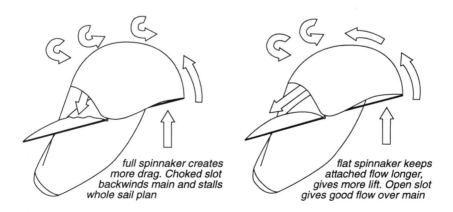

full spinnaker creates more drag. Choked slot backwinds main and stalls whole sail plan

flat spinnaker keeps attached flow longer, gives more lift. Open slot gives good flow over main

Fig. 1   *Different shapes of spinnakers produce different flows over sails.*

it may have chords that are deep in the middle and flat on the leeches like a V; or it may have chords that are a combination, such as having a flat center and flat leeches with maximum turn a third to a quarter of the way in.

The mitres are controlled by the chord characteristics from top to bottom. If all the chords have equally proportioned depths, the vertical mitres will be even arcs. More likely they will vary. The center mitre may be full in the head, flat in the middle, and hook in a bit at the foot skirt. The quarter mitres may be flatter in the head and even out to a fair arc lower down.

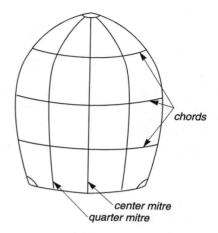

Fig. 2 *The overall depth of the sail is important and so is its shape.*

The proper lift/drag ratios and chord and mitre characteristics differ from one class to the next. Considerations include total weight and hull shape, lateral plane and design of centerboard and rudder, total sail area, pole length, crew weight and experience, and the courses you normally sail. If the class sets close reaches, your spinnaker must be able to sail high. If the reaches are never closer than 90 degrees, the sail can be built for carrying the pole off the forestay to maximize speed rather than height. For classes that can easily change spinnakers, there are specialized sails, typically a reacher and a runner. But for most one-designs, the spinnaker must optimize the variables and utilize the boat's strengths while compensating for her weaknesses.

Designing a given sail shape is one thing, but building a spinnaker that reflects that design when it is actually flying is something else. If sails could be made of tin, it would be easy, but we are restricted to woven material. In spite of recent advances in cloth development, the lightweight nylon used for spinnakers stretches significantly. Furthermore, it stretches more in some directions than it does in others. The least stretch occurs in the directions the threads run, the *warp* and the *fill*. The cloth stretches more and more as the loads approach an angle of 45 degrees to these threads (Fig. 3).

A design has to compensate for this stretch. Some construction techniques attempt to use the stretch factors and some attempt to minimize

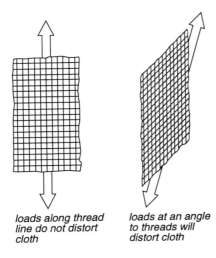

loads along thread   loads at an angle
line do not distort   to threads will
cloth   distort cloth

Fig. 3 *Though cloth stretch is
important, in all sail construction,
stretch along an angle that is at
variation with thread lines creates
the most potential for stretch.*

stretch. After trying both, I am convinced there is only one approach for racing boats over 15 feet long: to minimize cloth stretch with tri-radial construction. The alternatives, which are spherical or cross-cut, are much less satisfactory for reproducibility, longevity and predictability in varying conditions (Fig. 4).

There is a theory that a spherical spinnaker is good because it automatically opens the leeches in heavy air. On first thought, this sounds good. The bias is on the leeches, the bias stretches more than the thread line, therefore, under load, the leeches stretch more than the center, which flattens the sail and opens the slot. The only problem is that in the real world, every spherical spinnaker I have ever seen that has been used in heavy air has tight leeches. The bias of the sail itself stretches out just fine, but the leech tapes do not. Lightweight leech tapes, even no tapes at all with a double fold, do not stretch so much as the cloth inside the tapes. As a result, spherical spinnakers develop tight leeches, which are slow anytime. A crosscut sail stretches on either side of the center seam and develops what is called *elephant ass* which is not only slow but is also visually offensive.

I use cloth in the way it is most predictable - along the threadline. By aligning the cloth grain with the forces in the sail, one can minimize stretch variation from one lot of cloth to the next, one sail to the next, and through changes in wind and course. There are some myths about radial construction:

- *It is too flat, and you cannot make a good downwind sail.* Consider an orange which has a shape fuller than any spinnaker you would want. Score it in sections from the top down and you have a radial-head orange. You can put as much cloth in

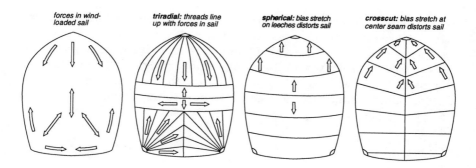

Fig. 4 *Spinnaker shapes have predictable loading areas. Construction must account for stresses.*

those gores as you want and cut it into as many gores as necessary to approximate a perfect shape.

- *It will be unfair or corrugated along the seams.* This happens only with improper broadseaming, cutting, or uneven tension in seaming. With practice and care, it is not a problem.

- *It is an overkill for a smaller chute.* I have seen spherical 505 and 470 spinnakers blow out in a single regatta; at best their peak competitive life is half a season. Tri-radial spinnakers last longer.

- *More seams make it heavy.* Actually, a tri-radial can be built out of lighter cloth, with equally good results, and this can reduce total cloth weight by as much as 40 percent. It lifts more easily in light air and is easier to stow.

I feel that many of the modern high-performance classes would benefit from flatter, or at least more precisely controlled, shapes. The modern developments in cloth and construction techniques make it possible to build such sails. But there is one catch. The flatter-entry spinnaker that relies on attached air flow is more demanding to fly. It requires constant adjustment of both sheet and guy to keep the flow attached. And when a flat sail is overtrimmed, the boat will go more slowly than one with a full sail which just sits up there fat and happy. But when a flat sail is trimmed properly, it will outperform the easy-to-fly chute on any point of sail in all conditions.

There's one more important thing to remember. You can buy a spinnaker that won this or that National or Worlds or whatever and you can read forever on how to sail with it. But to take full advantage of your spinnaker equipment in all conditions takes lots of practice. The more you sail, the easier it is for you to obtain boat speed and the more time you have left to concentrate on the race. So read about how to fly a spinnaker and also have good sails.

V

New Sail Materials

Speed and Stamina

*New sailcloths are changing
the way sails are made*

Jeff Spranger

If your impression of sailmaking is one of a sailmaker in kneepads scuttling around the loft floor, seemingly engrossed in an art form, then you probably haven't been to a sail loft recently. Nowadays, sailmaking is no more an art form than is synthesizing electronic music. It's a scientific process, involving computerized cloth testing and sail-shape design, computer-guided laser beams that cut panels, and sail "cloths" that are at the forefront of chemical and weaving technology.

Cloth. The building of the modern sail via computerized design and construction is in part a result of developments in sailcloth. Without access to a wide variety of cloths whose special characteristics and reactions to loading can be predicted, using a computer to design and cut panels would be impossible. Controlling and predicting what happens to cloth when subjected to loading – at locations such as the head, tack, clew, and reef points – lie at the heart of the evolution.

Four basic cloth fibers are used in modern sailmaking: nylon, polyester (Dacron), Kevlar, and Spectra. All of these can be and are used alone, but often two or more are used in a composite construction that takes advantage of the virtues of each.

These fibers can also be laminated to a film of Mylar (polyester extruded in sheet form). The Mylar film helps give the cloth the stability that simple weaving, even when done tightly and then treated, cannot give. Early Mylar laminates tended to break down with use, a problem that makers of Mylar-laminated sails are still trying to live down. Today, improved adhesives and cloth construction herald the arrival of much-improved durability.

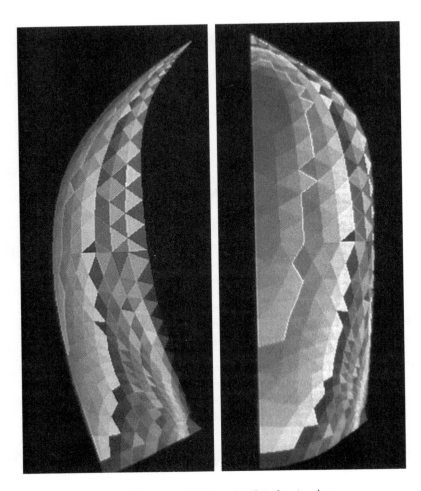

Photo 1 *Pressure distribution modeled on a North Sails spinnaker, viewed on a computer from two angles. From this, and from stress and strain programs, cloth requirements can be determined.*

Dacron.   Each of the materials for working sails has virtues and vices. Dacron, for instance, is relatively inexpensive but degrades in sunlight and tends to stretch. It holds a dye well. Dacron can be tightly woven, resinated, and heat-treated to improve the stability of the weave. These processes help Dacron sails retain their shape, but it is the inherent flexibility of the fiber that allows very old sails to last long after their shape is gone.

Kevlar.   For its light weight, Kevlar is remarkably strong and resistant to stretch. Sails made with Kevlar fibers have unbeaten shape-holding ability over a wide range of wind conditions. Also – and especially important on large boats – a large Kevlar sail can be handled by the crew, while a Dacron sail, typically heavier by one-third, can't. The reduction of weight aloft also improves a boat's stability. On the negative side, Kevlar is even more susceptible than polyester to ultraviolet (UV) degradation, and, worse still, Kevlar fibers break quickly when flogged or abraded.

Combining Kevlar with Dacron improves Kevlar's flex and chafe resistance and lessens the chances of catastrophic failure. Coatings can improve Kevlar's resistance to UV radiation, but only at the expense of weight.

Another approach is to use more Kevlar fibers than necessary for the strength required in a particular sail, in effect overbuilding the cloth to prolong its life. For some owners of larger boats, this may be worthwhile.

Spectra. A polyethylene variation that has the primary virtue of Kevlar – a high strength-to-weight ratio – Spectra also has a Kevlar vice, high cost. Spectra has one distinct and important advantage over Kevlar, the ability to withstand continual flexing. It does continue to stretch, or "creep," over the life of the sail, however, as Dacron does. Spectra is more resistant to sunlight than Kevlar. Allied Chemical, Spectra's manufacturer, claims a UV degradation rate no worse than that of Dacron. Spectra cannot be dyed, but it is white.

Laminates. As important as fibers are to woven sailcloth, it is their ability to be laminated that is crucial to their effectiveness as high-tech sailcloth. By laminating one or more plies of woven cloth or individual strands of fiber to a Mylar film, the cloth becomes more stable in directions not along the zero- and 90-degree thread lines.

Sailmakers and cloth manufacturers alike doubt if a modern laminated sailcloth, for all its decided improvements over early laminates, will last as long as simple woven Dacron (see table). Their aim, therefore, is to produce laminated sailcloth that will give significantly better performance and hold its optimum shape longer than woven Dacron.

One way sailmakers are looking to increase a laminated sail's life is by using a polyvinyl fluoride film called Tedlar in place of Mylar. It's heavier and not as stretch-resistant as Mylar, but has better UV resistance.

Both Dacron and Kevlar are well suited to laminating. The first (exceedingly slippery) versions of Spectra did not bond well, and this flaw stigmatized it. The same slipperiness made plain woven Spectra highly unstable on the bias, or diagonal, since the threads slipped and elongated as they passed over and under each other. Now Spectra is treated to improve bonding, and there is reason to take a closer look at the material.

Current applications. Spectra does seem to have much to recommend it for large sails. As with Kevlar, its light weight – two-thirds the weight of Dacron for a given strength – is a decided advantage.

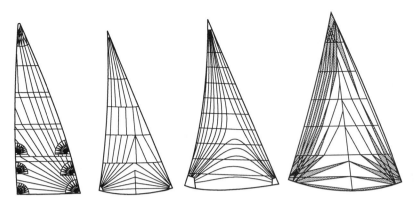

Fig. 1 *Lines of development: At left, a full-batten IMS mainsail from Hood, with Spectra leech reinforcement and Dacron forward, both Mylar laminated. Next, a Kevlar/Dacron genoa for grand-prix racing by Shore. This Mylar-laminated sail has several weights of cloth among its many load-oriented panels. Second from right, UK's Tape Drive genoa puts Kevlar tapes along principal load lines of the chosen laminate, which can therefore be lighter than normal. Right: Hild's Kappa Cut uses overlapping four-sided panels to minimize bias stretch and thereby maintain its shape over a wide range of wind strengths.*

There are notable exceptions to the view of Spectra as strictly for the large cruising boat. Some sailmakers say the performance of Spectra sails is at least equal to that of Kevlar and the durability far superior.

Yet it seems the high-visibility developments in sailcloth remain in Kevlar. Relatively new cloths include North Sail's Gatorback cloth and Dimension-Polyant's X-Ply. Both cloths are made by adding Kevlar threads at an angle to the basic thread lines of a standard Kevlar cloth. The angled thread adds strength on the bias.

The ultimate sailcloth is one custom-manufactured for a specific sail. Experiments for just that have been under way at sailmakers Sobstad and Shore. In Sobstad's Genesis process, threads are oriented individually along projected load lines on a roll of Mylar. Initially, Genesis has proven the more production oriented of the two methods. Sobstad's Pete Conrad thinks gluing technology will eventually make woven, sewn sails a thing of the past.

Clearly, sailmakers face an acute dilemma. The sails they sell certainly provide improved performance, but at what price? At present, any savings achieved in the design and cutting of sails by using computers is offset by the higher costs of the sailcloth. Right now, the only advantage the buyer has is that the competition for fewer new sail buyers has forced many sail lofts to keep prices so low that they are working on the barest of margins.

Some see the solution to the dilemma in making sails with "longer life and middle-of-the-road performance," which can come from improved adhesives and weaving. Equally important are sailors becoming more sophisticated and hence having higher expectations about boat performance and what it costs to achieve it.

Photo 2 *Spectra: Excellent racing results so far; cruising outlook better still.*

Material weight in oz	New strength, lbs/in.	1-month strength, lbs/in.	Loss, %
Dacron, 7.8	460	288	40
Soft Norlam, 7.0 (laminated Dacron)	325	220	32
Kevlar, 5.8	690	364	47
Spectra, 8.8*	700	700	?

Materials in North Cloth samples tested before and after one month's exposure to the sun in Florida. The samples are all (except Spectra) candidates for the same sail. Other factors, such as stretch and abrasion resistance, must be considered as well.

*The Spectra was too slippery to be clamped securely in the test machine above 700 pounds.

Courtesy North Sails

Table 1 *Degradation of sailcloths in sunlight.*

Up at the Leading Edge

*Leading sailmakers talk about their
new products and designs*

Charles Mason

━━━━━━━━━━━━

There's no question that the time-tested woven-Dacron headsail, built for years in the traditional cross-cut manner, still has its supporters, particularly among cruising sailors. But newer fabrics and the modern construction methods have produced a new generation of sails that are lighter, stronger, and just as durable as all-Dacron sails.

There was also a time when sails were built for cruising and for racing, but not both. Here again, the new fabrics have gone a long way toward eliminating that distinction; many of today's sails deliver excellent performance as well as durability and ease of handling.

To learn about these new developments, I asked three leading sailmakers to discuss the headsail they would build for a 38-foot cruiser/racer with the following general dimensions: the boat displaces 16,000 pounds, is masthead-rigged with a mast height of 47 feet, and has a *J* measurement (the base of the foretriangle from the mast to the headstay) of 15 feet.

With this sail plan the headsail is the main driving force of the boat when it's going to windward, and its performance has a lot to do with how fast the boat sails through the water and how easy it is on the helm.

The husband-and-wife owners, and perhaps one or two children or another couple, sail the boat on weekends. They plan on a two-week summer cruise with family and friends and an occasional club race to keep up their competitive skills. I asked the sailmakers to create two sails for the boat, each a 135 percent genoa. One would be designed to work well in both a cruising and a racing environment; the second would be tilted a bit more toward performance.

Even though all three sailmakers agree on the sails' functions, they come to somewhat different conclusions. In the end your local sailmaker's reputation for quality and service may be the deciding factor for you. But in the meantime, here's what is going on up at the front of the boat.

UK SAILMAKERS' OPINION

The husband and wife who sail this boat, perhaps with another couple, require a sail that is light, durable, and able to hold its shape over a wide range of conditions. Their principal concern is pleasant sailing, as opposed to violent exertions on the foredeck.

Although tri-radial construction is a viable alternative, we favor Tape-Drive construction to get a strong and light sail. A light sail is easier to set and douse; it takes less tension on the furling line to roll it up; the sail rolls up with a smaller diameter; it blows through the foretriangle faster in a tack; and it is easier to trim in after tacking. It is also easier to stow and to carry ashore. All these considerations are important to a cruising sailor.

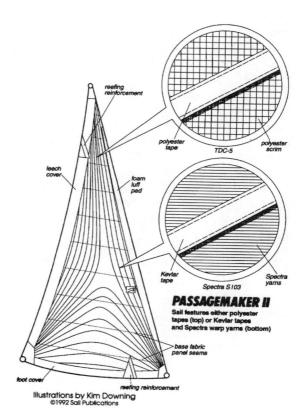

reefing reinforcement

polyester tape   TDC-5   polyester scrim

leech cover

foam luff pad

Kevlar tape   Spectra S 103   Spectra yarns

PASSAGEMAKER II
Sail features either polyester tapes (top) or Kevlar tapes and Spectra warp yarns (bottom)

base fabric panel seams

foot cover   reefing reinforcement

Illustrations by Kim Downing
©1992 Sail Publications

The sail we would recommend is made using a lightweight cross-cut base fabric laid out in panels that are sewn together. The fabric, called TDC 5, is a balanced polyester medium-density scrim, laminated to a layer of 1.5-mil Mylar and a layer of light polyester taffeta. The fabric weighs about 4.25 ounces per yard. This cross-cut construction provides excellent control over the set and shaping of the sail.

Load-bearing tapes aligned with the computer-predicted stress paths are then attached to the base fabric. Because the tapes are continuous and terminate in the corners of the sail, all the yarns in the tapes are load-bearing. Because the base fabric seams don't carry a load – the tapes do that – seam failure is very rare, and seam creep is eliminated.

Converging the tapes at the corners of the sail also eliminates the need for heavy corner patches. In a tacking situation, a soft, light, flexible corner isn't as apt to strike as hard as a sail with a big clew patch. The result is reduced potential for chafe.

We would recommend a roller-furling system for this couple. We would design the leech and foot dimensions to give the sail a clew height that is high enough to allow good visibility when the sail is used with roller-furling gear and low enough to the deck to be an efficient #2 genoa for racing when the furling drum is removed and the sail is tacked to the stem.

A foam pad along the luff keeps the rolled sail uniform in diameter so the unrolled portion sets smoothly. Reefing reinforcements along the foot and the leech help absorb additional loads on the reefed sail. A sacrificial UV-shielding cover along the leech and foot will screen out the sun's rays when the sail is furled.

For an owner who may want better stability from a sail that is even lighter, the same basic construction features apply, but with different materials. In this case the base cross-cut fabric would be a Spectra laminate called SI03, and the load-bearing tapes would be Kevlar yarns with a polyester fabric backing. SI03 consists of layers of 1.5-mil Mylar and light taffeta between which five heavy Spectra yarns per inch are inserted in the warp direction parallel to the seams. The Spectra fabric handles the loads in the warp direction, while the Kevlar tapes support the primary stress loads. This fabric weighs 3.3 ounces per yard, which is almost 30 percent less than TDC 5.

Assuming reasonable care, both sails should have a life expectancy of at least four or five years, and probably a good deal more.

— *Owen Torrey for UK Sailmakers*

SOBSTAD'S OPINION

The jib these owners need is the archetype of today's configurations. It must be able to perform in light winds as well as fresh ones. It must be able to withstand a lot of abuse and still retain its smoothness and beauty. And it must also be modestly priced.

Emphasizing a sail's light weight as a performance factor is a bit of a travesty that's been created by some sailmakers; the reason is that a sail's dynamic stability takes precedence over weight. And the weight of a sail, no matter how heavy it is, is only a fraction of the total weight of the mast, boom, and standing and running rigging. The real test of this sail, which will weigh about 40 pounds, is that it is light enough to be efficient in true-wind speeds that are as low as 5 knots, but also performs well in true-wind speeds of over 18 knots.

One fact of life with an overlapping headsail like this one is that the rig will be hard on the sail. Collisions with the shrouds and the forward

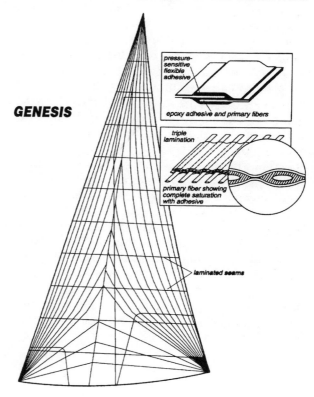

GENESIS

pressure-sensitive flexible adhesive

epoxy adhesive and primary fibers

triple lamination

primary fiber showing complete saturation with adhesive

laminated seams

side of the mast whenever the clew is released for a tack or gybe can inflict tremendous damage to the aft section of a headsail. That's why this area needs to be strong and very resistant to impact and abrasion.

Further, subjecting each side of the sail to the tension and compression loads created by going onto a new tack creates the potential for a number of things to happen. Film can crack, adhesive can break down, laminations can fail, and fibers can be severed. Fighting these problems from the strength side is only half the battle. The other half involves making a serious effort to make the sail's back end, or leech, strong and quiet. A properly laminated leech overlay can accomplish both missions perfectly.

For these owners, we would recommend using a Mylar/Tedlar/Mylar tri-film fabric for the basic structure, or membrane. A computer-controlled instrument then puts down on the membrane polyester yarns of 4,000 denier in the high load areas and 1,000 denier in low-load areas. The construction is then covered by 4×4 500-denier polyester scrim to improve the sail's resistance to tearing. Another reinforcing layer of scrim is attached to the membrane in the aft sections of the sail, in the leech area, to prevent damage from chafe, impact, and flogging. Reinforcing layers of the same-weight polyester scrim are laminated to the primary membrane in the tack, head, and clew areas to create the corner patches. The panels are laid out so that all the yarns are joined within the seam, which is then laminated, to make a virtually continuous fiber running from clew to head.

All these laminates are installed by applying urethane, polyester, and epoxy adhesive and applying heat and pressure to the area that is being laminated. We believe that a lamination provides far more strength than a sewn supporting structure.

For a higher performance sail, the only change we would recommend would be to use different yarn on the membrane. For more stability we would substitute an Aramid (Kevlar) yarn for the polyester yarn. The fact is that once any sail has been designed for a specific boat under this system, there are no additional "packages" required except for small details like draft stripes, numbers, and the like. A durable, attractive, and modestly priced cruising sail has the same requirements as one dedicated to racing. While tacking eyes, telltale windows, and the like can be, and probably should be, installed to help the racing crew, the basic stability and durability of the sail are still what is most important.

Both these sails should last at least three years without any noticeable reduction in performance.

— *Peter Conrad for Sobstad*

NORTH SAILS' OPINION

These owners' priorities, in order of importance, seem to be ease of handling, durability, performance, and cost, while an all-out racing sailor would put performance ahead of durability. For this cruiser/racer, we would recommend the Offshore Plus, a radial construction that is built with several weights of Soft Norlam. This fabric has a thin layer of Mylar sandwiched between two layers of Dacron, which gives it the feel of traditional Dacron but the shape-holding characteristics of a high-tech fabric.

Soft Norlam is warp-oriented, so it is perfect for a radial sail. Aligning six-ounce fabric with the high loads at the leech of the sail eliminates leech stretch. Using five-ounce fabric along the luff encourages some stretch and makes the sail responsive to halyard tension. Placing five-ounce fabric on the foot also produces some stretch so that sheet-lead adjustments are more effective. Although tear and chafe are always a problem at the spreaders, Dacron continues to be the most chafe-resistant material available.

Roller-furling is a good option here even though the gear uses up about two feet of the sail's luff length. A six-ounce layer of Soft Norlam with UV protection should be added along the leech and foot if the sail is to be used with roller-furling.

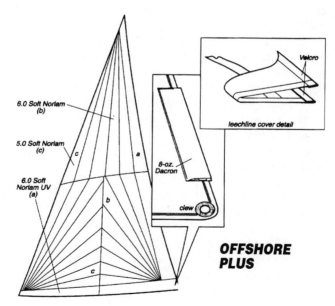

For a slightly more racing oriented sail, the next step up is a Spectra Club Racing jib. Note that this sail should not be roller-furled. Spectra's advantage over Kevlar, the fiber used in high-end racing sails, is that it doesn't weaken or fatigue from flexing, flogging, tacking, or UV exposure.

This fabric has Spectra yarns in the principal warp loads, with a polyester fill and a light Mylar film to provide stability, and tear and chafe resistance. Gatorback Kevlar yarns laminated on top of the Mylar film handle any additional stresses that occur during tacking. This sail is constructed with two horizontal seams instead of the single seam on the Offshore Plus. The two seams allow the Spectra panels to be narrow near the leech, and the thread lines don't have to be rotated as much at each seam; higher-tech sails would have three, or even four, seams.

Other specific considerations that might affect the final design of these sails include the shape of the boat's keel, rudder, and hull; the angle of the deck tracks off centerline; backstay adjustment and resulting headstay sag; and the maximum available hoist.

Neither sail will change much during the first two seasons. In the third year, the draft may go slightly aft and the leech may get rounder. But most cruisers will not even notice, and in most cases the shape can be restored completely. Both sails will remain structurally sound for at least several more years. A cruiser could get 10 years from these sails, until they literally fall apart.

— Perry Lewis for North Sails

light Kevlar or Mylar scrim (b)

head detail

Spectra 65TX (a)

luff tape

SPECTRA CLUB RACER

a

b

c

5.0 Soft Norlam (c)

The Amazing Mainsail

*Sailmakers say the workhorse sail
requires new grooming*

Charles Mason

Almost 50 years ago, a sail made of polyester made its debut on a sailboat. That fabric had been woven of a polyester fiber developed during World War II as a by-product of oil refining. More sails made of the fiber followed and proved far superior to the cotton sails that were then in vogue. Polyester sails lasted longer, didn't mildew, and held their shape far better.

As the years went by, the cotton sail faded quietly into the history books, and today sails made of Dacron (the name for the fiber in the United States) continue to be the first choice for a large number of cruising and racing sailors. Dacron fabrics are being constantly improved with state-of-the-art weaving and finishing techniques.

To be sure, there have been any number of other innovative developments in sailcloth since that first polyester sail appeared. Among these are low-stretch Mylar films and a whole range of laminated fabrics that use Kevlar, Spectra, and even carbon fiber in their construction. In fact, a recent survey found that more than 550 different fabrics are now being used in sailmaking.

Even so, Dacron remains a popular choice of fabric for mainsails. At least, that is what I found when four of the country's leading sailmakers talked about the mainsail they would suggest for a husband and wife who own a 38-foot cruiser/racer that displaces 16,000 pounds, is masthead rigged, and has a mainsail with a 41-foot, 6-inch luff and a 14-foot, 3-inch foot. The owners, with perhaps one or two children or another couple, sail the boat on weekends and take a two-week cruise in the summer. There's also an occasional club race during the season to keep up their sailing skills and retain bragging rights.

These four sailmakers say such a mainsail should be constructed of Dacron. It's durable and easy to shape and maintain.

Your own sailmaker may well have his or her own ideas about how your boat's mainsail should be constructed. Those observations, along with the ones that follow will go a long way toward giving you the inside track on the latest thinking about this very important sail.

NEIL PRYDE SAILS' OPINION

Since this couple is not going to be doing any serious racing, their first priority is to have a sail with good all-around capabilities. That's why we suggest an all-Dacron mainsail. Dacron will provide good performance and will last longer than a comparable Kevlar composite main.

Of course, if the racing program does start to take precedence over cruising and daysailing, this basic main should probably be reserved for use as a recreational or "delivery" main, which will extend the life of the all-out composite racing main they should use when their priorities change.

The basic mainsail for this couple, we suggest, should be a Cruise mainsail. This sail is built from Bainbridge 8.7-ounce high-tenacity Blade fabric: the name comes from the cloth's high thread count and excellent stability when it is loaded up on the bias. Such a sail is constructed in the traditional cross-cut fashion, with all panels laid out at 90 degrees to the leech.

Ultraviolet (UV) degradation and flogging can break down a mainsail. However, in this case the total annual UV exposure for the main will probably not be more than 200 hours. That amount won't have an adverse effect on the integrity of the fabric for many years.

Flogging, however, is a different story. Constant fluttering of the fabric breaks down the resins used in the finishing process and, in time, will affect the yarn itself. This will lead to a migration of the draft toward the back of the sail, creases at the inboard end of the batten pockets, and, eventually, fabric failure.

The good news is that the batten options available today help reduce this hard flogging and add to a sail's longevity. That is why we suggest that all four battens be, on average, about 15 percent longer than the "conventional" batten length that is allowed by most racing rules. Having full battens may affect your rating under some handicap rules. Be sure to check. We also recommend having one set of reef points. Cross-cut construction

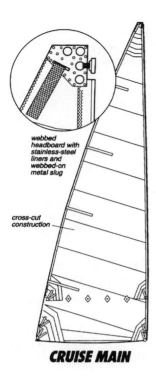

webbed
headboard with
stainless-steel
liners and
webbed-on
metal slug

cross-cut
construction

CRUISE MAIN

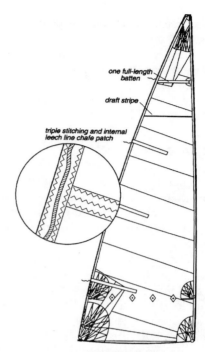

one full-length
batten

draft stripe

triple stitching and internal
leech line chafe patch

CRUISE PLUS

makes any shape deformation that may take place smooth. It also produces a sail without wrinkles or the "bias" bumps you sometimes see in a radial main of this size. Other important construction details on this sail include three rows of stitching on all seams and Dacron block patches throughout.

For a slightly higher performance sail, we suggest a Cruise Plus main. It's also made with a 8.7-ounce high-tenacity fabric, but we recommend adding a number of features to improve performance and further increase the sail's life expectancy. These features include a full batten at the top of the sail and longer battens in the other three locations. Long battens help reduce flogging along the leech and also make the sail easier to handle.

We suggest that this sail have a two-ply radial overlay at the head and at the clew. These overlays should taper into the body of the sail, and each overlay should be 25 percent of the length of the leech. Radial overlays extend and disperse evenly into the body of the sail the high loads that exist at the corners and make those corners virtually impervious to failure.

It is interesting to note that even though this kind of sail involves a lot of new thinking about how to handle the loads in the high-stress areas, the basic sail design, excluding the fabric, is pretty similar to the constructions we used 15 years ago. This Dacron main will provide at least two years of good racing performance at the club level and will, with normal care and use, last at least 10 years.

— *Bob Pattison for Neil Pryde Sails*

HILD SAILS' OPINION

When it's time to buy a mainsail, the first question is always whether to buy a sail made from a laminate for lightness and increased performance over a wide range of wind conditions, or to buy a Dacron design for that fabric's proven durability. If there is a cruising priority, these owners should think first about a Dacron mainsail.

We recommend a Performance Dacron main made with panel sections that rotate the thread lines. This enables the shaping seams to parallel the wind flow, which helps make the sail flatter as the wind comes up and the sail loadings increase. We like the top two battens to be full length and the two lower battens long enough to support the roach, but not so long as to interfere with the shaping of the lower part of the sail. Two full-length battens produce the stabilized draft of a full-batten sail, yet such a sail can also be shaped with the cunningham and flattening reef.

We recommend that the sail have radial patches at the head, the clew, and the luff and leech ends of the two reefs. Radial constructions distribute the load evenly into the corners, which is very important at the head of the sail because that area receives the highest loading of any part of the sail.

For good downwind sailing we suggest including a lensfoot, an elliptically shaped piece of cloth that is attached along the foot of the sail. Off the wind this additional cloth will allow the sail to be shaped as though it were loose-footed but will still allow the sail to retain the end-plate effect of the boom. We suggest two sets of reef points for the kind of sailing this couple does.

If this couple decides that racing is more fun than cruising, they might consider a Kappa Cut main. Such a sail provides the performance of a laminate without the durability problems of Kevlar. The Kappa Cut main is not built like a traditional tri-radial mainsail, where panels of triangles radiate outward from the corners. In a tri-radial construction one edge of every panel has to be cut across all the strong warp yarns, which creates a weak bias. A Kappa Cut sail, in contrast, uses overlapping parallelograms to maintain thread integrity within the panel.

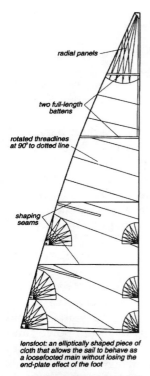

radial panels

two full-length battens

rotated threadlines at 90° to dotted line

shaping seams

lensfoot: an elliptically shaped piece of cloth that allows the sail to behave as a loosefooted main without losing the end-plate effect of the foot

PERFORMANCE DACRON

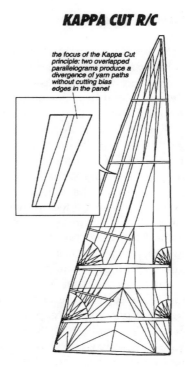

KAPPA CUT R/C

the focus of the Kappa Cut principle: two overlapped parallelograms produce a divergence of yarn paths without cutting bias edges in the panel

Since the uncut yarns are also oriented along curves, they react to sheet or halyard tension by becoming straighter under load. As the wind builds, the leech flattens and the draft of the sail moves forward and gets flatter. The overlapping-panel construction eliminates the need for heavy corner patches, with the result that cloth weight can be reduced from 8.2-ounce Dacron to 6.7-ounce laminate.

Of course, weather conditions and intensified use may shorten the life of any sail; however, a mainsail that is handled properly could last as long as 15 years. It all depends on the sailor. However, if the inboard ends of the battens are hinged or have wrinkles, there are vertical stretch lines between the battens along the leech, or the sail won't get flatter when the halyard or outhaul is tensioned, chances are it's time to go out and get a new mainsail.

— *Clarke Bassett for Hild Sails*

DOYLE SAILMAKERS' OPINION

That couple needs a mainsail that is easy to handle but still performs well. When they are cruising, the sail is being hoisted and occasionally reefed by a small crew. For the basic sail we suggest a Dacron crosscut CM 2+2 with two full-length upper battens and two lower battens that run halfway from the leech to the luff.

Since there is little performance benefit from full-length battens in the lower part of the sail, the half-length lower battens make the sail lighter and easier to handle. One problem with full-length battens in the lower section is that the leech falls first when the sail is lowered and the outer end of the batten reaches the boom first, leaving the forward end in a "batten-wedge" position several feet above the fully lowered position.

While cross-cut construction may not seem as high-tech as a radial layout, it is best for a Dacron mainsail. We recommend a tightly woven, balanced-weave 7.7-ounce Dacron, because a weave with the yarns packed close together prevents stretching along the diagonal, or bias, which causes sails to become fuller over time. We also recommend two sets of reef points. They do add to the cost, and some sailmakers recommend only one set for coastal cruising. However, our experience is that when you want a second reef, it is usually too windy to make sufficient headway under power, and the boat will not handle well with a partially furled headsail. A main with a second reef will provide control that is important when the wind begins to freshen.

We recommend eliminating the headboard on this sail because the full-length top batten makes it unnecessary. And a headboard tends to chafe the sail cover.

For a slightly higher performance mainsail, we would stay with a Dacron sail with two full-length top battens. But we suggest that this sail be constructed with a different base cloth – a high-performance square-weave Dacron originally designed for small one-design boats that also produces very good results on larger boats. This seven-ounce cloth is the same weight as that in the basic main, but it is a balanced weave with very tightly packed yarns to minimize diagonal stretch.

To further enhance performance and handling, we suggest tapered battens, which reduce weight aloft. These battens also improve shape control because the tapered inboard end allows the front half of the full batten to follow the sail's designed shape, while the stiff back half helps maintain a flat, open leech. The two tapered lower battens help promote a smooth transition at the inboard end of the batten pocket. We also suggest install-

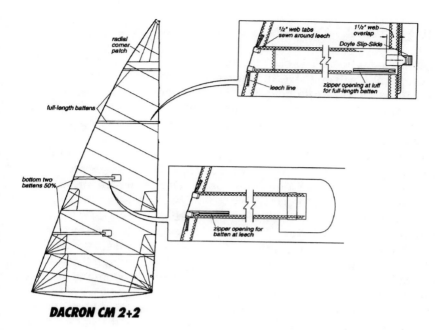

radial corner patch

½" web tabs sewn around leech

1½" web overlap

Doyle Slip-Slide

leech line

zipper opening at luff for full-length batten

full-length battens

bottom two battens 50%

zipper opening for batten at leech

DACRON CM 2+2

ing an overhead leech line, which runs from a fixed point on the clew up the leech to turning blocks at the head and down to a luff cleat at the gooseneck.

If they receive proper care, both these sails should last anywhere from eight to 12 seasons, depending on the amount of use they get. Proper care means putting on the sail cover whenever the sail is furled, taking care of any small tears or chafe points, and inspecting and washing the sail at least every two years. In time any sail will start to change shape. One of the most obvious changes is that the draft will start to move from the front of the sail to the back, which reduces performance. When this happens the sail can be recut to improve its shape, but many performance-oriented sailors make this the time to replace their sail.

One way to check the health of the cloth is to push a pin through the Dacron. If it "pops," it is probably still all right. If it doesn't pop, you should have the sail checked by your sailmaker. Another pretty good rule of thumb is that if you are spending over $250 each year for repairs to your main, it's time to think about getting a new sail.

— *Tom Erskine for Doyle Sailmakers*

HOOD SAILMAKERS' OPINION

Everyone who sails should understand that the mainsail has to be the most durable sail on the boat. Since it is set in practically all wind conditions, it has to be able to hold its shape throughout a very wide wind range. It must also be able to stand up to prolonged luffing conditions, which may occur, for example, when motoring with the sail up in a congested or narrow passage.

We recommend Dacron fabric and a cross-cut panel configuration, which, from our experience, is the most durable. For this boat we would use non-resinated Hood 7.5-ounce soft-woven Dacron, which makes a sail that is easy to handle. This fabric has an unbalanced weave with large, low-stretch, high-tenacity yarns in the fill, or vertical, direction and smaller, more twisted yarns in the warp direction. This construction produces a sail that has minimal distortion in the leech area, allowing sail shape to be adjusted through a wide range of wind conditions. Even though the sail will stretch as the wind increases, the fabric allows it to stretch and recover repeatedly when the mainsail is reefed, for example.

We recommend standard length battens for this sail. Although full-length battens make sail handling easier, they also make the sail more expensive and heavier, and full-length battens create more wear and chafe at points where they cross shrouds and running rigging. We recommend having an additional layer of Dacron fabric at each end of the batten pocket to keep the pocket and stitching from being chafed from the inside. We also suggest installing elastic at the inboard end of the batten pockets to keep battens under tension. We would add two additional layers of Dacron under the leech tape for additional batten-chafe protection.

We recommend having two sets of reef points. We believe that the first reef should reduce mainsail about 10 percent; the second, another 15 percent.

Sail reinforcements are also important parts of the sail, and we feel that a cross-cut sail requires cross-cut patches. We recommend Dacron reef patches to distribute the sheet loads gradually into the sail. Radial patches are correct for radial sails but are designed not to stretch, and we believe they can cause bias distortion in the area immediately adjacent to the patch.

If these owners decide to put more emphasis on racing, we suggest our Spectra/Mylar-laminate main. It is a far more powerful main than the Dacron cross-cut and weighs about 40 percent less. Its construction is bi-radial, which means that the panels radiate from the head and clew of the sail to spread the loads. The high-strength, low-stretch Spectra fibers are placed in the warp of the fabric, and the Spectra panels are aligned parallel

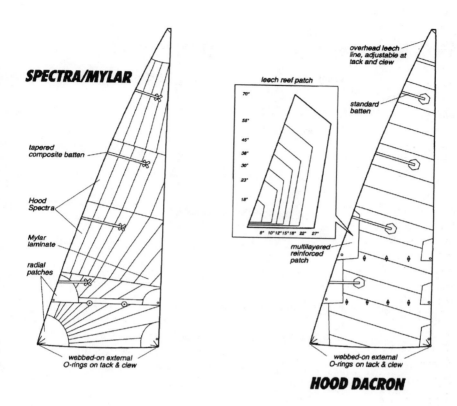

SPECTRA/MYLAR

tapered
composite batten

Hood
Spectra

Mylar
laminate

radial
patches

webbed-on external
O-rings on tack & clew

overhead leech
line, adjustable at
tack and clew

leech reef patch

standard
batten

70°
55°
45°
38°
30°
23°
18°

8" 10"12"15"18" 22" 27"

multilayered
reinforced
patch

webbed-on external
O-rings on tack & clew

HOOD DACRON

to the leech, where high loadings take place. Batten lengths on this sail would be the same as with the cross-cut main, although we suggest using tapered composite battens.

For both sails, we suggest applying penetrating coating on all exposed stitching for enhanced longevity and lower potential service cost. This application turns each stitch into a rivet, so even if the stitching is chafed away, the remaining thread cannot be sheared apart. For Dacron sails, a UV coating is also available and is recommended for any boat sailing in tropical waters. This coating can increase the life of the fabric by 20 to 30 percent.

While the life of any sail is always determined by how it is used and the treatment it receives, our Dacron sail should last a minimum of 10 years; our Spectra/Mylar sail, at least five years.

— *Tim Woodhouse for Hood Sailmakers*

What Goes Into Sailcloth?

Knowing their characteristics will help you choose the fibers for your sails

Peter Mahr

Almost every piece of modern sailcloth begins life as an industrial fiber. While the brand names of many of these fibers are well known, their basic properties are less well understood. The characteristics of these fibers may be the deciding factor when you choose a material for your sails.

The most important property of any fiber used for sailcloth is its *initial modulus*, which is its inherent ability to resist stretch. To account for differences in fiber weight, initial modulus is expressed as *grams of load per unit of stretch* for a given amount of fiber weight. Weight is normally expressed as denier weight, the weight in grams of 9,000 meters (29,520 feet) of a fiber.

A sail made from a fiber that has a high initial modulus will stretch less than one made from a material with a lower initial modulus. This assumes that both the sailcloth manufacturer and the sailmaker have extracted maximum performance from the fiber.

The search for a higher initial modulus has been the driving force that has taken the sailmaking world from cotton to Dacron to Kevlar and, more recently, to experiments with carbon fiber. Each improvement in initial modulus has produced sails that can perform in wider wind ranges and have improved overall performance.

The second most important feature in a sailcloth fiber is *breaking strength*, which is determined by dividing the load required to break the fiber by the denier weight. Although this figure is important, as a practical matter the calculation isn't used very often, because sails are typically much stronger than they need to be to withstand the loads placed on them. However, a fiber's breaking strength can be reduced by the flexing of the sail, ultraviolet (UV) degradation, and perhaps chemical attack.

Different fibers lose strength at different rates by different means, which is why different tests are used to determine exactly how fibers react. UV (ultraviolet) resistance, for example, is tested by exposing samples to sunlight and then measuring their breaking strength as they age. Using actual sunlight takes a very long time, so to reduce testing time, cloth samples are put in an intense-light chamber that speeds up the breakdown by about 100 times. However, since the light in the testing chamber is not natural sunlight, the accelerated tests may not be completely fair for all materials. Nevertheless, light chamber testing is the basis for almost all UV data.

Flex strength is another important sailcloth fiber feature. Basically, it is a fiber's ability to retain its strength after being folded back and forth. In the "50 fold test," a cloth sample is folded 180 degrees back and forth over a dull knife edge 50 times, and the strength loss is then measured. A complicating feature of the fold test is that the design of a piece of cloth can have a big effect on its ability to withstand fatigue and therefore on the test results.

For example, early Kevlar materials used tightly woven, highly resinated fabric in which the Kevlar fibers were locked in place. The result was that there was a 100 percent loss of strength in the 50-fold test. Since then, Kevlar laminations have solved much of the problem by keeping the fibers stable but allowing them to move very slightly (on a microscopic level) to reduce damage.

Although resistance to chemical damage isn't usually a problem with many sailcloth fibers, aramids (Kevlar, Technora, and Twarron) and nylon can be damaged by strong cleaners, particularly chlorine bleach-based agents. Keep this in mind whenever you clean your sails, and never be tempted to rinse your sails in a swimming pool.

Tear strength, which is a combination of fiber breaking strength and sailcloth design, is another important factor. However, since design is a very important factor in a fiber's performance, a comparison of individual fibers is rarely helpful.

A fiber's cost is important, although this often comes down to a question of value. A costly fiber may be worth the price if it can win more races or last longer than a cheaper one. The higher cost of a high-strength, high-modulus fiber is partially offset because it is possible to use a lighter sail, which means using less fiber. Unfortunately, high-strength fibers aren't yet so effective that they can be used to produce cheaper sails.

Photo 1 *Conventional spinnaker cloth uses nylon, shown here at a 90 times magnification. The cloth's design makes the fiber weave as flat as possible to minimize airflow through the fabric.*

One notable exception to this rule is sails for very large cruising boats. These sails once needed two and three layers of Dacron to make them strong enough to be good performers. Those labor-intensive sails have since been replaced by cheaper single-layer Spectra sails.

The fibers by name.
Polyester was developed in the early 1950s and is used for upwind sails because it stretches less than nylon. It is strong, durable, and relatively inexpensive. It is made by a number of manufacturers. Perhaps the best known name in sailcloth is Dacron polyester, made by Du Pont, whose high-tenacity, low-stretch type 52 Dacron was developed specifically for sailcloth. Other polyester fibers are called Terelene, Teteron, Trevira, and Diolene by their manufacturers.

Nylon is used for spinnakers because of its light weight and strength. Nylon's stretch is not as big a disadvantage in spinnakers as it is in mains and headsails, where nylon is never used. Some contemporary spinnaker cloth is made from special small-denier polyester yarns. They have lower stretch but do require expertise in manufacturing and are less forgiving of mistakes in sail trim. A collapse with a polyester spinnaker could be a problem in a breeze, because the fiber's low stretch won't allow the sail to refill without a risk of breaking. Nylon is more susceptible to UV and chemical degradation than is polyester sailcloth.

In 1980 America's Cup boats first used Kevlar, another Du Pont fiber, in a laminated form. This fiber has high initial modulus and breaking strength. It is stronger than steel for its weight and is five or more times as stretch-resistant as polyester. However, in sunlight Kevlar loses strength about twice as quickly as polyester. Flex-strength loss is also more significant. Careful handling and minimizing the flogging of a sail can greatly extend the life of Kevlar sails. Leech flutter is another cause of breakdown; adjusting the leech cord quickly can help preserve Kevlar sails.

Almost all Kevlar sails use type 29 Kevlar, which is available in different deniers. The process used to make Kevlar fiber results in higher performance-to-weight ratios for small fibers than for larger ones. For example, the difference in initial modulus between a 400-denier fiber and a 1,500-denier fiber is 22 percent. However, the 1,500-denier yarn is also much less expensive, which is why less-costly Kevlar sails have well-spaced strands of larger fibers; grand-prix sailcloth tends to have many more small fibers.

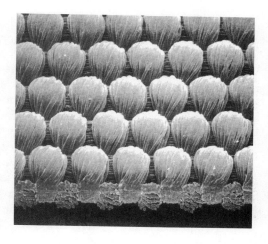

Photo 2 *Traditional sailcloth like this is made of tightly woven fibers of polyester. The larger fibers, shown at a 30 times magnification, run horizontally and are called fill fibers. They carry the heavy leech loads of a cross-cut sail and, because they have low stretch, are not bent like the warp fibers, which are woven at 90 degrees to the fill fibers.*

There's also a type 49 Kevlar, which is used in rigid structures like boat hulls and also in maximum-performance sails, such as those for America's Cup boats. It is 50 percent higher in initial modulus than type 29, although this comes at the expense of some flex strength and a higher price.

Type 129 and type 159 Kevlar are also available on occasion for sailcloth. Type 129 falls between type 29 and 49 in initial modulus and is a bit stronger but also more expensive. Type 159 has a slightly higher durability, but it is also more expensive than type 129 and is available in only a few deniers.

Kevlar was developed by Du Pont in the 1960s, and two other companies now have products based on similar chemistry and processes. The generic term for these fibers is *aramids*. Akzo in Germany makes a yarn called Twarron that is similar to Kevlar and is often used by European sailcloth makers. Another aramid fiber, called Technora, is made in Japan by Teijin. This fiber has a slightly different chemistry and the same or slightly lower initial modulus than Kevlar 29. It also has slightly better flex-test results but noticeably worse UV resistance. Flex differences between

Technora and Kevlar are small compared to those between the different cloths that can be made from them. Technora comes in two colors - a natural gold color and black. While the black is better than the gold for UV protection, light-box tests indicate that it is not as UV-resistant as Kevlar.

In 1983, Spectra was introduced by Allied Signal as a possible replacement for Kevlar. A highly processed version of polyethylene, Spectra has good UV resistance, very high initial modulus, and excellent breaking strength. However, it does have a property called *creep*, which is a tendency to elongate under sustained load. This can result in a change in sail shape as the sail ages. Spectra is very popular on larger cruising boats where strength, UV resistance, and durability are more important than the last fraction of a knot of boat speed. Spectra costs about the same as Kevlar.

Vectran fiber is entirely different from the aramids and Spectra. It is an LCP (liquid-crystal polymer) and is a distant relative of polyester. Vectran has a modulus similar to Kevlar 29's, but suffers no strength loss from flex. This means it lasts longer in such endurance applications as the Whitbread Round-the-World Race. This capability has been proven by the Whitbread Maxi *Merit Cup*, which has used an all-Vectran sail for two years with a strength loss of only 15 percent. A Kevlar sail would be expected to lose about half its strength in the same period.

The bad news is that Vectran presently costs 30 to 50 percent more than Kevlar, and its UV resistance is lower than both Kevlar's and Technora's. This means that you must take extra care when exposing a Vectran sail to sunlight. The cost will undoubtedly come down when the fiber is produced in greater quantities.

The America's Cup. The 1992 Cup races broke new ground when the Italian challenger, *Il Moro di Venezia*, hoisted a set of sails containing carbon fiber, and the *America*[3] defenders followed a week later with their own version, which they called "liquid crystal" (even though the fabric was actually a hand-laminated combination of Spectra and carbon).

Carbon fiber has an extremely high initial modulus but is not very durable. If you try to fold a raw fiber between your fingers, it will snap before you complete even one fold. Carbon has enjoyed varying degrees of success in sailcloth, but in all cases the sails must be handled very carefully to avoid any folding or hard creases. While future America's Cup syndicates may continue to explore carbon development, the high cost and inherent fragility of the fiber will limit its use to only the best-financed syndicates.

New fibers are constantly being developed by the major chemical companies and are being evaluated simultaneously by sailcloth manufac-

Photo 3   *A typical Kevlar sailcloth, shown at a 90 times magnification, has the Kevlar fibers, shown in the 150 times magnification inset photo, cut off and facing outward. The fabric is designed so the polyester fibers are woven across the Kevlar fibers, which holds them straight and keeps them in place. A Mylar film and lamination adhesive run across the bottom of the weave.*

turers and sailmakers. While the developments we've seen so far are exciting, they are by no means the end of the development of new fibers. In fact, the one thing we all know for sure is that more innovation in fibers and construction is on the way, and that, in turn, will produce better and longer lasting sails.

Proper Mylar Maintenance

*Increasing a sail's longevity makes
dollars and sense*

Peter Mahr

To understand how to care for a Mylar sail, it is important that you know
how the material is made and how it is meant to perform. In most cases,
Mylar sailcloth consists of a light woven cloth glued to a thin polyester
film. This film, called Mylar when manufactured by Du Pont, is made from
the same plastic as Dacron sailcloth. It is strong and stretch-resistant and
resists chemicals, temperature, and sunlight well. These properties, together
with the inherent stability of film, make it ideal for sailcloth.

Mylar by itself makes a strong but very fragile sail. Bonding cloth to
the film provides tear strength for the composite and adds strength and
stretch resistance in the thread directions. Conventional Mylar sail material has a cloth substrate that is made of either nylon or Dacron polyester.
Both materials perform well, but the polyester has a little extra resistance
to sunlight degradation and chemical attack. It is impossible to tell which
material your sailcloth has by examining its pattern because the nylon and
Dacron are both woven in a stop-rip pattern, like spinnaker cloth, and in a
plain weave, like genoa cloth. In either case, sail care is the same except for
special cleaning methods.

The chemical compositions of the adhesives that join woven cloth to
the film are closely held secrets and vary widely among sailcloth suppli-
ers, so it is impossible to say much about them. Some early adhesives had
bad faults such as turning brown with age or losing their grip when they
became wet. Current adhesives are good enough so that we do not have to
worry about them when considering how to handle a sail.

Mylar sailcloth has changed since it was first tried. The original styles were not very flexible and tore easily, but new constructions have significantly reduced both these problems. Now the tear strength of some Mylar materials is actually better than that of the conventional Dacron cloth they replace. The flexibility of the new styles is probably comparable to that of normal racing sailcloth, and it is better than that of the coated fabrics that are used in high performance one-design sails.

The first question you, as a new Mylar sail owner, will face is, How do I store the sail, rolled, folded, or stuffed? It is now standard practice to fold a Dacron sail because woven cloth breaks down minutely every time it is creased. Folding minimizes the amount of breakdown by reducing the number of creases that result when the sail is stored stuffed in its bag. Fortunately, Mylar sailcloth does not break down with creasing as woven cloth does, so this problem is less important to the life of the sail.

The material does wrinkle, however, so simply stuffing it into a bag makes the sail pretty ugly if the next set happens to be in light air. But the creases caused by folding do not significantly affect light-air performance, and they pull out as the breeze freshens. Folding, then, is still the recommended procedure for bigger sails (Fig. 1). One-design sailors who are already accustomed to rolling up their sails and storing them in tube bags probably should continue to do so with their Mylar sails in order to avoid wrinkles completely. As always, don't forget to dry your sails before they are stored.

Proper boat preparation is important to save all your sails from tears. Even though the newest Mylars are less subject to tears than the Dacron they replace, nothing is indestructible, and your boat should be checked carefully for sharp objects. Look for uncovered cotter pins on the turnbuckles, spreader tips, and spinnaker pole fittings. If anything is question-

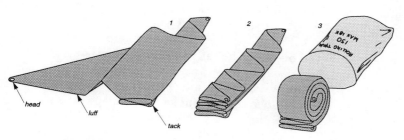

Fig. 1 *This accordion-like procedure is best for folding large sails of Mylar-laminated fabric.*

able, wrap it with duct tape, file it smooth, or cover it up. A little care here will pay off many times.

In use, Mylar sails are not much different from Dacron sails, except that they are less forgiving of mistakes. The most important rule for a Mylar sail is: *Never exceed the sailmaker's maximum wind speed recommendation.* The vast majority of Mylar sail failures can be traced to ignoring this rule. Mylar sails hold their shape so well that people find they are still fast at the top of their range. It can really slow you down to change from a new Mylar light #1 genoa to an old Dacron heavy #1, but if the wind is up to the limit, you have to change.

The first step in protecting your sail against overload is to make sure you get good wind speed maximums from your sailmaker before you take the sail out the door. It is an excellent idea to stencil this speed on the sailbag and also to write it on the clew in indelible marker so the crew or a guest skipper can also find this information quickly. The next step is to check your anemometer with some reference you think is accurate. If you doubt the accuracy of your wind gauge or don't have one, be sure you are conservative when you make your sail selection. The final step, of course, is never to get caught with the sail up too long as the wind is increasing. Don't try holding on for the last mile with a few knots of extra breeze.

It has always been possible to ruin a conventional light genoa by carrying it beyond its range. But the result is far less obvious with Dacron than it is with Mylar. Overloaded Dacron genoas get blown out as the cloth finish breaks down, and the result is a slow sail. Overloaded Mylar sails usually wind up with broken seams, separated clew patches, or curly leeches, all of which are hard to ignore.

If you do get caught with a light sail up in gusty conditions, it is possible to prevent destruction by easing the sheet off and reaching off during the puffs. This technique, however, is no substitute for making the proper sail change when you should.

Similarly, you should follow your sailmaker's advice on halyard tension. Normally Mylar sails are set properly when there is just enough halyard tension to remove the luff wrinkles. Excess halyard tension can distort the shape and even overload the sail in the head or tack areas. If you have hanks on your Mylar sail, be sure to use only enough halyard tension to remove the crow's feet wrinkles around them. Too little tension with hanks can cause high point loading and can locally damage the sail.

Do not let a Mylar sail flog excessively when you are setting it and tacking, although Mylar suffers less from fatigue than does woven Dacron cloth. Beating against rigging is very destructive to any material, and the loads caused from flapping can also be high. The noise level created by a flogging Mylar sail is also very high.

Good crew work is always important during tacking, but it becomes even more critical when you have a Mylar sail. Never let the sail backwind hard against the rig. If the breeze is up, you are asking for a split sail. To provide a little insurance against this happening, spreader patches are a must. You should mark the spreader position on the sail and have your sailmaker install the patches as soon as possible. Don't forget that changing the rake of your mast can move the spreaders enough to miss the patches, so check the fit after any major mast retuning.

To increase tacking speed and save the clew of the genoa from beating against the mast and shrouds, use a tacking line. This arrangement consists of a grommet pressed into a patch halfway along the foot of the jib. A tacking line extends from that point through a block at the bow and back to the cockpit. This line also can be the spinnaker foreguy if it leads to the bow (Fig. 2).

Tacking requires good coordination between crew members on both the sheets and the tacking lines. In a tack, release the old sheet as usual and haul the tacking line in to pull the sail forward. Once the bow has passed through the eye of the wind, release the tacking line and take in the new sheet. In light air a crew member could walk the clew around the mast so it doesn't hang up on the shrouds.

Chafe can be a problem when sails rub against pulpits, lifelines, and spreaders. Because many Mylar sails are so light, they are more susceptible to chafe than are the Dacron sails they replace; therefore, it is important to minimize contact wherever possible. If there is a point, perhaps at the base of the shrouds, that is rubbing continuously, fit a patch on the sail where it rubs for added protection. On a boat where the sail rubs all along the foot,

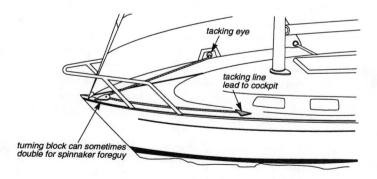

Fig. 2 *A tacking line is an excellent way to speed up passage of a sail past the mast, as well as to keep chafe to a minimum.*

the lower panels can either be made of a heavier weight material or be two-plied, with the cloth side facing out to provide extra strength.

Sunlight always has been destructive to sailcloth. Sails never should be left exposed for extended periods. Materials containing nylon are worse than those containing polyester, so for a sail used in the Caribbean, Florida, and other intense sunlight areas, select a cloth with a polyester substrate material if possible.

A preventative maintenance program will go a long way toward making your Mylar sails last. Have your sailmaker check the sails after your season is over to look for small holes and tears, weak seams, and so on. During the season, periodically inspect all the seams, particularly along the leech and at the end of the largest clew patch. The highest loads in the sail occur at the edge of the clew patch; this area also takes a lot of abuse during a tack. If you find that the Mylar is breaking around the stitching, have your sailmaker repair it *immediately*, before the break is complete and a real problem develops. A two- or three-inch-wide Dacron adhesive-backed tape, called insignia tape, stuck over the seam, particularly the last patch seam, will greatly increase the seam's strength – and therefore the sail's life.

The tape adheres so well that it does not really need to be sewn down. But stitching it on wouldn't hurt as long as the stitching isn't near the tape's edge. For a highly loaded sail on a big boat a three-inch-wide tape overlapping the seam three feet in from the leech on both sides of the sail will help avoid seam failures. Where the tape sticks to the shiny film side it is completely effective. It doesn't help as much on the cloth side, so a two-ply sail, which has cloth on both sides, is harder to reinforce after it is built.

While repairing Mylar sails is pretty straightforward, only your sailmaker should mend them. Small holes the size of an ice pick point can be ignored. Larger holes can be repaired temporarily with sail repair tape, but large rips should be repaired properly. Fortunately, it is relatively easy to match the performance of the Mylar cloth in the patch with that of the sail because stretch is unaffected by use and the variation in performance between different production runs is very low.

Separation of the cloth from the Mylar, called *delamination*, can be caused by severe overloading, weak seams, or point loads. If delamination occurs, the problem area can be replaced by your sailmaker and the sail restored to its top performance. You should not continue to use a partially delaminated sail because the damaged area will only grow and the loose Mylar can tear.

After a couple of seasons your sail may start looking a little dirty and you may get the urge to clean it. The best advice for all sails, including

Dacron genoas, mains, and nylon spinnakers, is to ignore the dirt. You can reduce the performance of the cloth with a vigorous washing. If you simply cannot stand the unclean look any longer, use a mild detergent with lukewarm water and be sure to rinse all the detergent out afterward. Mylars made with nylon cloth can become even more sensitive to sunlight if any traces of acid remain in the cloth. Never use bleach, any acidic cleaners, or chlorinated water (as in swimming pools) to clean these sails.

All this talk about rips, chafe, overloading, and sunlight degradation might sound negative and scary. In fact, sailors have always faced these problems with racing sailcloth, and Mylars aren't really all that different.

Mylar sails can save a racing sailboat owner money not only by lasting longer, but by performing over a wider wind range; this can reduce the number of sails in a complete inventory. Mylar does make sense, and it is here to stay. But any racing sail must have constant care and attention if it is to remain at its peak racing potential.

Trimming the Mylar Headsail

Looking good is also good for performance

Steve Cruse

████████████████

The end product of the years of research and development that went into today's Mylar headsails is an unquestionably faster sail. But the reason it is faster is often misunderstood.

The tremendous advantage of a Mylar sail is that it can work in an extremely wide range of wind strengths when it is trimmed efficiently and correctly. A Mylar genoa can perform well even when it is poorly set and sheeted. But 10 to 20 percent of the sail's potential won't ever be realized unless the trimmer makes frequent use of three simple trimming tools: halyard tension, sheet-lead position, and backstay tension/headstay sag. The trimmer uses these tools to *shift gears* when either wind or sea conditions change. Optimum pointing ability and speed through the water will be achieved only when these trimming tools are used correctly for the existing sea and wind conditions.

Because each tool has an infinite number of settings, the trimming procedure can be confusing. I suggest that you limit yourself at the beginning to three settings of each trimming tool for any one headsail. Doing so will give you a quicker understanding of how one adjustment affects another in the particular conditions being encountered. I use settings that correspond to the most frequently used descriptions of wind and sea conditions: light, medium, and heavy.

Let's assume you are sailing a 35-foot racer/cruiser with an all-purpose Mylar #1 genoa. This all-purpose sail has an effective wind range of three to 18 knots. Your first trimming move is to set halyard tension. I should start by pointing out that the halyard of a Mylar genoa functions differently from that of a Dacron sail. Draft position in a Mylar sail is pretty much decided by the sail designer and cannot be moved around with halyard tension as it can be in the inherently stretchy Dacron sail. Instead, adjusting a halyard on a Mylar genoa radically alters the *leading edge* of the sail, varying the angle of attack of the genoa luff to the apparent wind direction. In other words, the amount of halyard tension you create determines your pointing ability. A slack setting produces a fine leading edge entry that is appropriate for light air and smooth water conditions.

To locate this setting on your boat, hoist your sail slowly and stop tensioning the halyard the moment all the wrinkles in the luff tape area disappear. Then ease the halyard off one inch and mark this position on your halyard (position A). Incidentally, making reference marks is essential for reproducing any successful setting. It is surprising how often this detail is ignored even on the best racing boats. With a Mylar genoa the total variation in the luff tension on a 45-foot luff (about the average length for a 35-footer) will be only three inches. Therefore, you should make another mark one inch tighter (position B), and a third mark (position C) one inch tighter still. If the jib luff is longer, total adjustment length will be greater than three inches; if it's shorter, it will be less.

The first position is suitable for smooth water conditions with three to eight knots of apparent-wind strength. The fine luff entry of this position permits high pointing. In winds of eight to 12 knots apparent, sea conditions will require you to have a more rounded entry at the luff. You'll need a sail that stalls less easily because the helmsman now has to steer a wider course through the seas without stalling the genoa. This is the time to tension the halyard to position B. When the wind increases further to 12 knots apparent and you approach the top end of the range of the all-purpose #1, the sea state will increase along with the wind, which makes an even rounder entry necessary in order for the helmsman to steer effectively and still keep the genoa powerful. This is when you increase halyard tension to its maximum, at position C.

Increasing and decreasing halyard tension also raises and lowers the genoa up and down the sail plan and affects your second trimming tool, the genoa lead position. To start, find your *average* lead position (setting B) by sailing to windward in 10 knots of apparent wind. Adjust the genoa lead forward of aft until all three luff telltales break at the same time. Obviously this position also becomes the genoa lead location for halyard position B, which is the proper tension setting for beating in a medium sea and medium apparent wind strengths.

If wind and sea conditions allow you to lower the jib halyard to position A, your genoa lead will probably be too far aft at this setting. The reason is that easing the halyard lowers the sail and, in turn, lowers the clew height. Therefore, move the genoa lead forward 1.5 inches to setting A to avoid over-twisting the sail at the upper part of the leech. An over-twist depowers the sail exactly when you want to have power.

Increasing halyard tension from position A to position C for the heaviest winds therefore requires that the genoa lead be moved to setting C, three inches aft of setting A. Whenever you are increasing halyard tension on a close-hauled course, always ease the genoa sheet to avoid over-trimming the sail and closing the upper leech. The best way to observe this phenomenon is to watch the leech of the sail move toward the spreader when halyard tension is being increased. In fact, if the genoa sheet were not eased, the spreader could poke into the sail and possibly damage it.

The last tool, and probably the most important in terms of power generated, is backstay tension and, thus, headstay sag. I like to think of the knob on a hydraulic backstay panel as my power throttle; it should be adjusted constantly through all light and medium wind ranges. Once again, I'll use the three settings A, B, and C to illustrate. Hydraulic adjusters, incidentally, are extremely reliable and provide the complete adjustability of backstay tension and headstay sag that is necessary to achieve 100 percent of the performance designed into a Mylar genoa.

Increasing headstay sag is comparable to adding sail area to the jib luff and produces a fuller and more rounded forward shape. Therefore, an eased backstay creates a powerful round shape forward, the shape that is required in a medium or heavy choppy sea.

For our 35-foot racer/cruiser example, let's designate as setting A the light-air setting of 800 pounds. With either smooth water or a medium apparent wind strength, double the backstay load to 1,600 pounds and mark this setting B. This flattens the sail – you don't need power in a smooth sea – and also keeps a consistent amount of headstay sag for the medium breezes.

At the top end of the wind range you want the flattest possible shape, and you get it with maximum backstay load, in this case setting C, at 2,400 pounds. Obviously, all the recommended maximum backstay loads for your boat must come from your boat's manufacturer. You should also understand that the gauge readout does not necessarily indicate what load is on the backstay. It could be just what the pump is experiencing. More specific conversion scales are available from the hydraulics manufacturers, and these scales can be attached directly to the hydraulic panel for ease of reading.

Effective use of backstay tension allows a trimmer to substantially alter the chord-to-depth ratios of the genoa and tailor the sail beautifully to specific conditions. With the genoa lead and the halyard tension set correctly, the backstay, along with the genoa sheet, can be played constantly to take advantage of the slightest variation in wind or sea. For example, when driving through a large powerboat's wake, you want to ease both the backstay and sheet to power up the sail.

To summarize the three tuning tools, halyard tension alters the sail's entry and therefore the boat's pointing ability. The jib lead should always be adjusted, along with halyard tension, to keep the luff telltales flowing and to maintain the proper leech twist. Finally, backstay tension affects the depth of the sail; you increase or decrease power as needed by adjusting it.

Of course, there will be times when you need to have settings that are not precisely A, B, or C. A case in point would be when you are sailing to windward in a moderate chop with eight knots of apparent-wind speed. Here you want the halyard at setting B to create a round entry, the genoa lead position at setting A with your sheet eased slightly for powered-up trim, and the backstay at position A for a powerful sail. In fact, in medium-to-rough seas, the backstay tension required will typically be one setting less than both the halyard and lead position.

Remember that to sail fast in all wind or sea conditions you have to change gears in order to keep getting optimum performance from your sail. Since these basic settings work with all your Mylar jibs, you may be able to put off making a headsail change if the tactics of a race require it. For example, easing the backstay from setting C to setting B and moving the lead forward a notch on the #2 genoa might be more effective than changing to the heavy #1 if you are approaching the windward mark.

Always note the combinations and conditions that have been successful against your closest competitors. And when you approach a leeward mark, don't forget to decide where to place the halyard, genoa lead, and backstay before you round the mark and go on the wind. You'll gain substantially over the boats that are still adjusting after the mark rounding. They may find a fast setting, but it will be well after you have powered away and are long gone.

VI

Gear Tricks

Powering Up the Full-Batten Mainsail

It's nothing new, but it works very efficiently

Steve Cruse

These days it seems everyone's talking about the "rediscovery" of the full-batten mainsail. Armchair sailors and sailmakers have developed catchy names for the sails, but whatever they are called, they are here to stay, both for racing and cruising – and for many good reasons.

The advantages of the full-batten main are many. The sail flogs less while hoisting, lowering, and tacking, making for quieter sailing. It also greatly extends the life of the sail, since flogging is a critical accelerator of breakdown in sail fabric. In a Mylar/Kevlar main, full-length battens can triple the effective and structural life span of the sail.

A full-batten racing main is usually built of lighter materials, which reduces weight aloft, reduces a boat's pitching, and increases its stability. Once the sail is retired from racing, it makes a wonderful cruising main because it is half the weight of an equivalent Dacron sail. The full-length battens fair in the shape of the sail, making it more efficient. The performance gains you can achieve on the wind when replacing an older cruising sail are often startling. Full-battened mains can have larger roaches. While sailing downwind, the full-length battens perform as whisker poles do, supporting the roach and projecting more sail area to the breeze.

Design. The full-batten main's design is different from a conventional sail in order to deliver all the potential performance benefits. When you're shopping for a full-batten main, be sure to ask your prospective sailmaker how the sail would be designed. Simply adding full-length battens to a standard design can compromise the resulting shape.

What does a full-length batten do? The batten prevents the roach from moving forward in all conditions, thus producing a better flying shape. With reduced fabric shift and roach movement, the main tends to hold the draft forward and also maintains a flatter shape as wind speed increases.

Because the battens support the roach, a compression load is created at the forward end of the battens. This can bend the battens in the forward part of the sail, affecting shape and therefore the luff curve. If the sail designer does not match the luff curve to the mast characteristics, a mainsail with excessive draft forward, especially near the tack, can result.

One popular misconception is that a full-batten mainsail develops higher performance only because of increased roach and increased sail area; in fact, roach is limited both by rating rules and the presence of the backstay. It is true, however, that adding more roach up toward the head of the sail and even reducing roach down low make a very efficient elliptical profile. (Fig. 1).

On most racing boats, a full-batten main is designed to the maximum allowable roach, and the roach could overlap the backstay by up to six or eight inches. Although the cruising sailor should avoid this configuration, the racer wants to have the highest performing sail allowed. A main that has this amount of overlap must have good chafe protection on the leech, because wear is going to be induced by contact with the backstay on every tack. Although the sail can be tacked through the backstay when there is a breeze, in light air it may get hung up. Often this hang-up can be solved by tensioning the cunningham and easing the halyard off a few inches.

For cruising boats under 55 feet, four battens are ideal. On bigger boats, five or six battens may be necessary to produce the desired sail shape. A good rule of

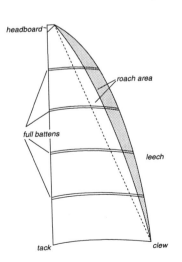

Fig. 1 *The optimal profile of a full-batten mainsail shows how the roach area along the leech of the sail is extended by full battens to provide a more efficient foil. The inside shape shows the roach profile of a mainsail not fully battened. The roach is defined as a straight line drawn from the outer end of the headboard to the clew of the sail.*

thumb for the larger cruising sail is one batten for every 12 feet of luff. Racing mainsails for boats under 55 feet are being built with just two or three full battens out of four. There are a couple of theories, however, on the right number of full battens.

Proponents of two full-length battens (at the two upper-batten positions) believe they produce an improved head profile but maintain more shape flexibility by keeping the lower two battens at the new International Offshore Rule legal length. A second advantage of the two full-batten configuration is less weight from the battens in the lower half of the sail. Although this point is valid, less weight comes at the expense of some durability.

A racing sail that has three full-length battens with the bottom batten about 40 percent of foot length allows for good draft control through cunningham adjustment without sacrificing durability and retains the projected roach-area advantage at the third batten down from the head.

Battens. The basic "pull-truded" fiberglass batten is virtually indestructible and is suitable for all cruising and most racer/cruiser applications. For more demanding racers, a variety of tapered battens utilize lightweight composite construction along with a distribution of flex. "Soft nose" (soft-ended) battens are even more effective when used on the partial-length #3 and #4 batten pockets. A high-tech batten can save you 50 percent in weight, but they can be relatively expensive.

New to the market is a round and hollow pull-truded fiberglass batten that has an excellent strength-to-weight ratio and uniform flex in all directions. The stiffness cannot be varied, however, as it can with a flat batten.

The round batten can rotate inside the pocket while the sail is being raised or lowered. If the leech is twisting, the batten also twists and doesn't transfer torque to the sail slide, which makes for reduced friction on the sail slides and easier hoisting and lowering. One drawback to a round batten is chafe from point loading, where the round surface makes contact with the pocket. A good example is where the batten pocket comes in contact with a shroud while you are broad-reaching or running.

Sail construction. In order to handle the compressive loads resulting from the push of the roach to move forward, the batten must be attached in some way to the sail slide at the forward end of the batten pocket. A heavy-duty webbing run through the sail slide, then hand-stitched to the pocket, makes a durable, flexible connection. Flexibility is critical, because in the case of a flat batten, the pocket might rotate 90 degrees when the sail is flaked. The webbing also makes an excellent chafe patch between the pocket and the mast.

Flat sail slides work best in all circumstances; slugs tend to bind. Round battens can help in some cases. The commercially available *Batt-Slide* is a good solution to problem installations. These fittings connect the batten to the sail slide by way of a stainless-steel universal joint that minimizes the torque loading of the sail slide or slug. In racing application, a bolt rope-style luff works quite well, providing the batten pocket is padded at the forward end.

Having the batten enter the sail at the forward end of the pocket makes for a clean leech with no extension that can catch on lazyjacks or running backstays. Obviously, the battens shouldn't be located where they lie directly against the spreaders while you are reaching and running, which makes for more chafe on the batten pockets.

Sail trim. The question of how to trim a full-batten mainsail always fascinates me. A properly trimmed full-batten main should achieve the same objectives as a standard main: proper fullness for the wind and sea conditions, along with a solid attached flow off the leech, determined by looking at the streaming telltales located on the leech at each batten pocket.

The only tricky part about the sail is that it tends to look good whether it is in trim or not. The sail tends to "smile at you." Use exactly the same trimming aids as you would with any mainsail. Depending on wind and sea conditions, the leech should be either sheeted in or twisted off to stream the telltales. Use the draft stripes on the sail to read adequate fullness and draft position. Halyard, cunningham, sheet, and outhaul tension have the same effect on shape as they do on a more conventional sail, although draft position is going to be a bit more "locked in" by the nature of the design.

Many sailors overtrim a main as they try to eliminate backwinding. Because the full-batten sail is a more semi-rigid foil than the short-batten sail, it takes slightly more easing on the sheet to produce a noticeable amount of backwind.

Similarly, when depowering a full-batten main in a breeze, the trimmer can ease both sheet and traveler down until the head of the sail is actually inverted, but still the sail will not be flogging. This quality is a tremendous benefit, because this profile creates far less drag than does a luffing sail. A depowered full-batten main doesn't disturb flow over the rest of the sail.

In lighter winds, you will find that stiff battens create a flatter shape than desired. In this situation, over-tensioning the leech line increases the compression on the battens, which, in turn, adds a curve to them and increases the depth in the sail. You can make more permanent shape adjustments by altering the flex characteristics of the battens; additional flex can be created by decreasing batten width in the desired area, usually the forward end. More stiffness can be created by taping a shorter and thinner batten to the main batten.

Although multihulls have been racing for years with full-batten mainsails, today's racers should thank the cruising sailors for the current popularity of the full-batten main. The offset is that cruising sailors have received the benefit of the improved technology that has come from the changes the racers have made to the design. Here's a situation in which it can be truly said that everyone wins.

Winging It with a Whisker Pole

It's almost like having an extra hand aboard

Art Bandy

If you've ever tried sailing downwind without a whisker pole for your jib, you know that stabilizing the sail is tough to do. A whisker pole is any pole attached to the clew or genoa sheet near the clew that is used when running off the wind to hold out the sail on the opposite side from the mainsail and keep the jib clear of the mainsail's wind shadow. Whisker poles can be of fixed length or telescoping. They come in various styles and with a wide range of end fittings.

What size whisker pole do you need? In general, the pole should be as long as the foot of the sail – the largest sail, if you have several jibs – but never less than 125 percent of the J measurement (the base of the foretriangle from the mast to the foremost stay on which the jib is set). Rating rules may affect this computation; if you use your boat for racing, make sure the length of the pole conforms to the rules. A telescoping pole can be used in a shortened condition with a small jib and fully extended with a bigger drifter or genoa. Here again, be sure the racing rules permit such a device.

Rigging. In general, the outboard end fitting of the pole should be attached to the jibsheet so the sheet will run freely through it. The only exception to this rule is on smaller boats, where a whisker pole may have a spike at the outboard end. The spike is pushed through the grommet at the jib clew or through the bowline in the sheet at the clew. When you gybe the jib, you must also gybe the pole – remove the spike from the jibsheet, let the jib come around, and reinsert the spike into the knot. Otherwise, you're likely to bend the end of the whisker pole.

On boats 25 feet or more, it is best to mount a mast car and track on the front of the mast so you can adjust the height of the pole above the deck. A working jib will fly at a different clew height than the genoa, for example, and poles always work best if they are kept level.

On a smaller boat, you can use a fixed padeye on the mast for the whisker pole. It's a good idea to mount two of them, one high and one low. No matter what size your boat is, remember to mount the track and car, or padeyes, in the center of the forward face of the mast so you can fly the pole to port or starboard from the same mount. Make sure the mast mount is properly sized to the inboard end fitting. If it is not correctly matched, the end will bind up, bend, or break. If there is any question, check with the manufacturer to make sure you have a proper mate.

Poles do weigh something, and they can pull down the sheet, which distorts the sail. As often happens on larger boats in light air, the weight can even pull the sail and pole down into the water. The solution is to attach a topping lift to the outboard end of the pole; a second jib halyard or an unused spinnaker halyard can serve as a topping lift to support the weight of the pole so it will not drag the clew down.

On some boats the pole may have a tendency to climb in the air, or "sky." You can install a line, or foreguy, that runs from the outer end of the pole to a snatch block at the deck or rail and then back to a cleat. If you want to keep things a little simpler, an option is to change the lead of the jibsheet and move the block on deck forward so the jibsheet pulls the pole down as well as back.

Trimming tips.   The "right" way to set and trim a pole varies from boat to boat and depends on the layout, standing rigging, and style of pole. Experimentation in light air is the best way to find the right procedure.

It's usually best to (1) snap the sheet into the pole's end fitting, (2) attach the topping lift, (3) attach the inboard end of the pole to the mast fitting, and (4) extend the pole outboard. Don't put tension on the sheet while you are putting it into the pole; any tension will make the setting more difficult as the pole fights you by wanting to lift or pull away.

It helps to have the helmsman *head up a few degrees* from direct down-wind *while you are setting the pole.* This makes your job easier by keeping the jib from flapping across the deck while you are forward and helping to stabilize the boat, preventing an accidental gybe. After the sheet is set in the outboard end and the inboard end is attached to the mast fitting, you can take up on the topping lift, tension the windward jibsheet the correct amount to bring the jib clew to the outer end of the pole, and square the pole to the wind as the helmsman heads off downwind again.

Downwind sailing with the main boom on one side and the pole on the other can be very exciting for the helmsman, who must keep the boat tracking on a straight course and avoid suddenly backwinding or gybing the boat. When you are running directly downwind, trimming is straightforward. What you want to do is to keep both the main boom and the whisker pole in a straight line across the fore-and-aft axis of the boat.

If the main boom is 90 degrees to the centerline on one side, the whisker pole should be 90 degrees to the centerline on the other. If the boat is not headed directly downwind, the boom should be trimmed in slightly and the whisker pole eased out so boom and pole remain parallel as much as possible. In fact, the trim varies from boat to boat. Shrouds can limit the amount you can bring the pole back and ease the main boom forward. Never pull a whisker pole back against a shroud; the pole may be dented and, therefore, weakened. Again, a little light-air practice will quickly tell you how far you can trim the pole aft or ease the main boom forward. Never set the pole between the forward lower and main upper shrouds because this greatly limits the amount of movement you can give the pole and increases the chances of damaging it.

Can you use a whisker pole with a spinnaker? The answer is a definite *"no."* Most racing rules don't allow it, but a more important reason is that a whisker pole, which is usually lighter than a spinnaker pole, is not designed to take the tremendous compression loads developed by a spinnaker. Spinnakers must be used with poles that are properly designed and configured.

Cruising spinnakers, which have become popular over the past several years, are usually made of light cloth and are used in lighter winds. Many are used without a pole. You can use a whisker pole with many cruising spinnakers as long as the tack of the sail is attached to the stem of the boat. Remember, however, that these are large sails; if you plan on using one on a long-distance passage that might take you through heavier wind conditions, be sure the pole is large enough to handle the additional loads without failing.

Easing Headsail Changes

Simple homemade devices are
sometimes a big help

Larry Montgomery

━━━━━━━━━━

Good sailors are always concerned about safety, but they are also interested in improving their seamanship skills. One particular area where it is easy to recognize a good sailor is in sailhandling and sail changing.

Changing headsails is an exacting practice any time. But in the dark or high winds, it can become difficult, occasionally even dangerous. At these times the possibility of crossing a sail hank, setting a sail upside down, or even losing some of the sail over the side to a boarding sea is a real threat.

But the great sailors seem to have the ability to swap headsails with apparent graceful choreography. My answer to preventing an awkward sail change lies in a simple device that works well with conventional sail hanks. Using it will make your sail changes safer and far more orderly. First, I'll explain how to use it; then I'll describe how to make one for yourself.

A sail often comes out of the bag in a confused heap. The device I use to ease sail changing is basically a wire rope pendant with a snaphook at the bottom, an eye at the top, and a plastic retainer at either end. When the sail hanks are attached to the pendant, they are easy to control.

The thimble and eye of the pendant should *always* be at the head of the sail, while the bronze snaphook is *always* at the tack. The advantage of this setup should be obvious. There is no longer any question, when you start to haul the sail out of the bag, about which end of the sail is which.

Furthermore, the entire series of hanks becomes instantly available at the top of the sailbag, and each hank is placed in its proper order.

In short, this device can do a number of things for you. First, it removes any possibility of crossing sail hanks. Second, it prevents even a beginner from setting a sail upside down. And finally, it allows you to set a sail just by feel alone, even in total darkness. By using this pendant, I find my sail changes go much more smoothly, and as a result, they can be completed more quickly.

Let's look at how the system works when, for example, I drop my genoa and replace it with a jib. First, I go to the mast and release the genoa halyard. I let the halyard slide through my fingers until I can feel a line marker that I have whipped onto the halyard. When I reach this marker, I know that the headsail has been lowered to the deck, and more important, I know the halyard shackle attached to the head of the sail is exactly 22 inches from the base of the headstay – the same length as my pendant.

If no crew is helping me, I cleat off the halyard at the mark, and with the genoa's empty sail bag in my hand, I move forward. First, I tie the sail bag, using the lanyard on its bottom, to the lifelines or bow pulpit. Next, I take the spare pendant from the sail bag and attach the bronze snaphook to a belt loop on my pants. The genoa sheets, because I will not use them with the new sail, are removed from the sail, neatly coiled, and dropped into the bag. Then the entire body of the sail is stuffed into the bag.

When the sail, except for the luff, is contained inside the bag, I remove the pendant from my belt loop and attach the snaphook to the shackle at the base of the headstay. Next I remove the halyard shackle from the head of the sail and attach it to the eye of the pendant. Then I start transferring the sail hanks from the bottom of the headstay, in order, to the pendant. After the last hank has been shifted, I secure the halyard's snapshackle to any convenient spot, usually on the bow pulpit, and I remove the pendant from the headstay base. The genoa luff, held in order by the pendant, is ready to be stowed. The final step is to put the pendant and luff of the sail in the bag, tie the bag, and stow it below.

The procedure is reversed for the new sail. The new jib is carried forward and the bag is tied to the lifelines. The snaphook of the new pendant is attached to the base of the headstay, and the halyard is transferred to the eye at the top of the pendant. The jib hanks are then transferred from the pendant to the headstay, starting with the bottom hank. After the last hank has been hooked onto the headstay, the halyard shackle can be transferred from the pendant to the head of the sail. Then the pendant is disconnected from the base and dropped into the bottom of the empty sailbag, and the bag is stowed. Once the new jibsheets have been led aft, the new jib can be hoisted.

Obviously, this sail-changing procedure may vary somewhat to conform to the needs of your own boat. The snaphook on the sail-changing pendant could be eliminated, for example, if you already have several shackles fixed at the base of your headstay. However, the concept of this system should be clear. Without such a device, you can be quite vulnerable once you have started removing your sail. Suppose you have taken off two-thirds of the hanks and then a breaking wave plunges you waist-deep in green water. The unattached portion of the sail can easily be swept overboard and the still-attached hanks torn loose. Recovering a wet sail that has gone overboard can be difficult, even in calm conditions. With this system the luff of the sail is captured at all times. And if an emergency should arise somewhere else on the boat, the entire sail-changing process can be delayed without fear of losing the sail overboard while you handle the problem.

My own sail-changing pendant is 22 inches long eye to eye and is constructed of 0.125-inch flexible stainless steel wire rope Nico-pressed around two appropriately-sized stainless steel thimbles. The bronze snaphook has a stainless steel spring, although a stainless steel snaphook also could be used. The plastic retainers, cut with a 1.5-inch hole saw, aren't really necessary if your jib hanks are small enough so they won't slide over the thimble and eye. I carry four pendants, one each for my staysail, genoa, jib, and storm jib.

This sail-changing device and the procedure that goes with it are a good example of how a simple piece of equipment can increase your onboard efficiency and safety. Obviously, it doesn't work with sails that are built to be used with grooved headstays. But in many cases, this system improves how you change your headsails. And it is a good way to enhance a good sailor's stock in trade: smart and crisp sail changes.

Jiffier Reefing

*These tips give new life
to an old-fashioned method*

Eric Hall

████████████

Jiffy reefing's simplicity and efficiency have won it almost universal acceptance since it first became popular. Boom manufacturers have changed
over from booms where the jiffy-reefing hardware was mounted externally
to models where it is rigged internally. Properly rigged internal-reefing
booms are an improvement, but they demand a different setup and different operating techniques from their external-reefing predecessors.

The new booms have no cheek blocks or padeyes attached to them.
Reefing lines are led through sheave boxes in the end of the boom and exit
near the gooseneck where they can be stopped off or cleated. One reason
for changing to this system is that it allows any boom to reef any sail regardless of the position of the aft reef point. With externally rigged hardware, the padeyes and cheek blocks must be positioned relative to the reefing cringle so that they exert the optimum combination of leech and foot
tension. If they are too far aft, foot tension will be fine but you will be
unable to get sufficient leech tension. Mount them too far forward and the
reverse will be true. Cringles are also placed differently in different
mainsails. The new system eliminates those worries.

Internal reefing also eliminates virtually all clutter from the boom.
There are no sharp cheek blocks or padeyes to take their toll on light sails,
clothing, and occasionally, your noggin. There are no reef lines drooping
down from the boom waiting to snag whatever or whomever happens to
be in the boom's path.

The general principles of jiffy reefing are the same with both internally and externally led reefing lines: jiffy reefing involves holding the luff

reef point down and forward at the tack by means of a line or reefing hook. A two-part reef line holds the leech reef point down and back and provides proper leech and foot tension (Fig. 1).

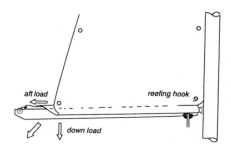

Fig. 1 *Jiffy reefing means holding the sail down at the tack and exerting proper tension aft and down on the clew grommet.*

With externally mounted reefing lines, a padeye on one side of the boom and a cheek block on the other are mounted approximately four-to-six inches aft of the reefing grommet so that the reef line pulls aft and down at approximately 45 degrees. The internally mounted lines achieve the same effect, but they do it in a slightly different way, and that's where problems can arise for sailors who don't fully understand how the new systems should be set up.

It is not immediately obvious how the leech-reefing line should be tied off. The inclination is to lead it from the sheave at the end of the boom and tie if off to the reef grommet. This, however, fails to provide proper leech tension. As a result the boom drops and the sail bellies out to leeward in an unseamanly and unsatisfactory manner.

The proper method is to take the reef line exiting from the end of the boom and reeve it through the reefing grommet in the leech of the mainsail then straight down to the boom where it is tied off. The line thus pulls aft to the sheave box and down to the boom. As long as the reef line is tied directly below or just aft of the reef point, the reef tension will automatically be optimum and no padeyes will be required.

The best way to tie the reef line off to the boom is through a foot grommet if the sail has a bolt rope in its foot, or beneath the foot if it is attached to the boom by sail slides (Fig. 2). To tie off, lead the reefing line from the clew grommet directly down to and through the foot grommet, under the boom, and bring it back and tie it to itself at the point where it enters the foot grommet. Use two hitches formed in a downward spiral (Fig. 3). Going around the boom and back up through the foot grommet causes the knot to pull into the grommet. Tying in a downward spiral will prevent the knot from jamming fast against the boom under tension as it should.

You can also tie off without a foot grommet by leading the reefing line from the sheave box, through the reefing grommet, down beneath the

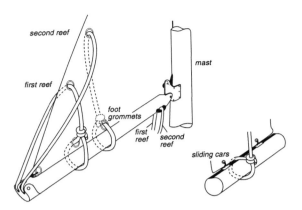

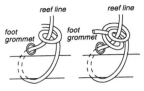

Fig. 3 *If you tie a hitch in a downward spiral, it will slip until pressure jams it against the boom. Then it will hold fast.*

Fig. 2 *Tie off internally reeved reefing line to the boom through the foot grommet when the foot of the sail is attached to the boom by a bolt rope. Tie the reefing line under the sail when the foot is attached by sliding cars.*

boom, and up around itself on the other side (Fig. 4a). This forms a self-adjusting loop that works well except for the large amount of friction it creates and the danger of the loop slipping over the end of the boom or into the sheet block. Another variation is to proceed as in the previous method but, rather than tying the bitter end around the line itself, reeve it through the grommet on one side, beneath the boom, and back up and tie it into the grommet on the other side (Fig. 4b). Friction and loop slippage are dangers with this method, too. Some sailors feel that they would rather add padeyes to the boom than grommets to their sails, and this works fine. However, I fail to see the point, and, given my choice, I'd rather be hit in the head by a clean round boom than by one bristling with padeyes.

Once you understand the theory, there are lots of things you can do to simplify reefing in practice. First, always leave the reefing lines set up. Internal booms are just as neat with the lines reeved as they are without. That's one of their beauties. If the wind increases suddenly and your reef lines aren't reeved, you are subjecting whoever reeves them to an unnecessary risk. Without messengers leading up to the reef grommets it will probably be impossible anyway. Rain or shine, rig the reef lines before you go out.

If your lines are set and ready it's easy to begin the following sequence. Take the steps in order and you should eliminate most of the difficulty from reefing. Perform any of the steps ahead of its proper slot, however, and you render the task extremely difficult.

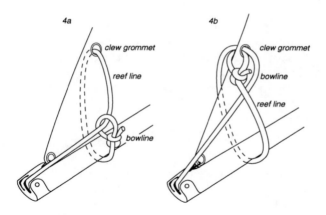

Fig. 4 *You can avoid putting foot grommets in the sail by tying the reefing line to itself as shown or to the clew grommet. You'll have more friction and a less secure position for downward pull, however.*

1. Ease mainsheet and vang.

2. Ease the main halyard with enough slack to hook the tack grommet easily onto the reefing hook. (Rings attached to a tape on either side of the reefing grommet are easier to hook over the reefing hook than the grommet in the sail (Fig. 5). The rings should be bigger in circumference than the grommet. You can fit a second ring over one already on the hook, reefing down without having to untie your first reef, which also makes it faster and easier to shake out a double reef and return to a single.)

3. Next, take up the tension on the mainsail luff by re-tightening the halyard. The topping lift should be positioned to keep the boom from falling to the deck during the reefing operation.

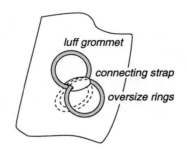

Fig. 5 *Anchoring the luff can be made more effective by adding rings that attach more easily to the reefing hook than does a grommet.*

4. With sheet and vang still eased, pull in the leech reef line from the gooseneck, securing it when the sail is pulled tightly to the boom. Instead of being adjusted at the gooseneck, some reefing lines are led back to the cockpit and once tightened, are held by sheet stoppers on the cabintop. With vang and sheet loose you should be able to tighten the reef line in almost any condition.

5. Trim the mainsheet and readjust the vang.

Don't wait until a big squall hits to try out your new, sure-fire reefing system. Nothing in sailing works without practice, so don't subject your system to its ultimate test until you've practiced with it. Pick a day when reefing isn't a necessity, make sure that your regular crew is well-briefed on the sequence to be followed, and then try it. Repeat it a few times until it goes smoothly. Then when you really do need to reef and you do it in 15 seconds with no raised voices, you and your crew can share the sense of satisfaction that comes from knowing that it really works.

Choose and Use Light-Air Sails

Here's the scoop on bloopers, thrashers, flashers and drifters

Sal Fertitta

████████████

Light-air sails with a host of names and shapes – drifters, bloopers, gennakers, thrashers, flashers – share a common ancestry with the spinnaker. Because their evolution has paralleled improvements in lightweight materials, they also share characteristics inherent in those materials.

The term *lightweight* has two connotations here: One indicates a light sail (typically a headsail) for light wind, and the other refers to a high-performance sail (including the mainsail) made of lightweight, generally exotic materials and used primarily for racing. Put another way, while sails for light air are always lightweight, not all lightweight sails are made for light air.

To further differentiate, light air sails of the first type are so-called specialty or non-working sails. Usually they are made of nylon that is improved with ultraviolet retardants, laminated with scrim for strength, and fabricated in multi-plies or bias cuts. The second type usually incorporates more exotic materials in composite structures or laminates of film and fabric in hybrid panels to improve the strength-to-weight ratio of existing working sails.

After you strip away all the trade names, light-air headsails generally fall into three categories: racing spinnakers (symmetrical), cruising spinnakers (asymmetrical), and all-purpose genoa-cut sails. Performance is based on a number of factors, so you need to understand and match the type of light-air sail you purchase to your type of sailing.

Racing needs are obviously more stringent than cruising ones, and sail usage varies. If you plan long passages where sails remain set for long periods, a reaching (cruising) spinnaker may be what you need. If you sail on weekends – out and back from your marina, changing your points of sail frequently – you may be better off with a genoa that can go upwind.

Most light-air sails for cruising boats combine nylon with scrim in either 0.75- or 1.5-ounce material. The more exotic laminates of films and aramid, even if cost-efficient, are primarily intended for racing. For instance, a medium- to heavy-displacement boat up to about 38 feet LOA, with a high righting moment would do well with a 0.75-ounce nylon reaching sail. For a boat longer than 38 feet, a 1.5-ounce fabric is a better choice and is in fact a wise choice for any boat that normally sails upwind.

How do you choose your sail? Visit lofts that concentrate on what you want: a racing or a cruising sail.

Evaluate the loft.   You can tell a lot by the way the shop is run, its efficiency, how the people react. Take a tour. If you are shown a computer, find out how it's used. Ask about the kind of warranty offered; a good loft always stands behind its product.

Evaluate the product.   A sail should be neatly sewn. Check seams for such signs of sloppy work as loose or uneven threads. Zigzag sewing with four or five stitches per inch is liable to chafe; seven stitches per inch is more durable. Look for tabling (reinforcing fabric) that is the same weight as the sail material; it should be stitched to give the thread something to hold on to. If the fabric is a laminate, check the scrim pattern for regularity. Good craftsmanship is apparent in triple stitching, overlapped and wider seams, and edges "tabled" with tape, not just folded and stitched.

Evaluate chafe protection.   Look for patches at stress points and chafe points, hank protectors, "butterfly" reinforcements at seam ends to spread the load, and oversized corner patches. The best clews are built up with layers of the same material, but perhaps of different weight, as the sail.

Regardless of the material from which they are made, there are two categories of light-air headsails: genoa types and spinnaker types.

Genoa types are asymmetrical sails, commonly called drifters, of smaller size than a #1 genoa and shaped the same. They can be designed either to be hanked onto a headstay or to be flown free like a spinnaker, yet they are handled like a genoa.

Spinnaker types are either symmetrical, with equal luffs and equal distance between clews, or asymmetrical, with the leech shorter than the luff to raise one clew higher. Asymmetrical or single-luff spinnakers are generally smaller and lighter for a given boat than a racing (full) spinnaker. They have a variety of shapes and are flown with one luff tacked at the bow or on a short, sometimes retractable, bowsprit. The panels are normally arranged in one of three ways: radial head for smaller boats and bi-radial or tri-radial for larger ones.

After you've bought your light-air sail, practice! Experiment with it, but always stay within the sailmaker's parameters. Learn to maximize the sail's advantages in wind under five knots on all points of sail. If the sail is attached to the headstay with straps or hanks, experiment with the tack height. For even wider adjustments, attach a pendant or downhaul to the tack and lead it through a block at the stem and back to the cockpit.

On a broad reach, learn how high (higher is usually better) to let the tack rise above the deck. On a dead run, try winging the sail out, with and without a whisker pole. Try to keep the sail out of the main's shadow, and ease halyard tension in small (maybe five percent) increments to let the head fly off to the point at which it is drawing efficiently.

With a genoa-type sail, hoist with enough tension to relieve loading at hanked points. Trim in to flatten the luff and see how high the sail can point. Also experiment with the sail flying free to learn how to tack and gybe it.

Trim tips.   A free-flying sail is flattened by increasing the distance between the clews; reverse this procedure to increase depth in the lower portion of the sail. With any hanked-on genoa-type sail, leech tension controls the head of the sail. Move the sheet lead forward to close the leech; move it aft to tighten the foot and flatten the sail.

Although it's hard to generalize because of the number of possible sail-and-track configurations in use, good starting points for drifter lead settings on a mid-sized cruising boat with short tracks are: for a dead run, full aft; for a broad reach, aft; for a beam reach, forward; for a close reach, far forward (hanks only).

A properly trimmed, poleless spinnaker should normally curl first at the shoulder above the centerline when you begin to sail high. A flying drifter (no hanks) gives the same signal by curling more toward the sail's center. My experience with symmetrical spinnakers is that I tend to "feel" when adjustments are needed and alter course to make them. With a drifter, I tend to "see" when adjustments are needed by observing the set of the sail, and I trim to course. Stress lines forming on a properly set drifter will tell you when it's time to lower it in the face of rising wind.

Care and maintenance.   Faced with compromises inherent in the construction of any lightweight sail, you must take good care of your light-air sail. Here are some dos and don'ts:

- Do keep track of wind force; don't overstress a light sail in heavy gusts.
- Don't let the sail flog. Even in light air, flexing is damaging to lightweight structures.
- Do rinse the sail periodically, preferably in non-chlorinated water. Salt deposits abrade.
- Don't store the sail wet; dyes in colored panels may run and transfer.
- Do preventive maintenance. Inspect for loose threads and chafe spots and tune up the sail at the loft at least once a year.
- Don't let the sail get near the spreaders; they are a sail's arch-enemy.
- Do bag or cover the sail when not in use; UV is another enemy.

Chafe is often ignored with light-air sails because the concept is a bit of a paradox. Light air seems to imply a lack of strength to cause meaningful chafe. Not so! All sails tacked to the bow and used on the wind can benefit from oversized, but light, patches at the tack and pulpit areas, at the first stanchion, and certainly at the spreader position. Light-air racing sails will have more patches, while off-wind sails that fly high and above the lifelines need fewer. But no sail is immune to chafe, seam stress, or puncture.

Finally, approach the purchase of your light-air sail realistically. It is not a gimmick. Although it won't move your boat when there's no wind, it does have a useful role in your sail inventory. Once you understand what a light-air sail can do for you off the wind, you'll find the improved performance is well worth the cost.

Handling a Three-Halyard System

*When lines are clear of each other,
problems disappear*

Bill Gladstone

───────────

The most common configuration for headsail halyards, particularly on racing boats of any size, is a three-halyard system (center and two "wings") and a twin-grooved headstay. This arrangement provides maximum flexibility and speed in changing headsails. The system requires the foredeck crew to keep the halyards clear at all times, which in turn means establishing simple procedures that are easy for all crew members to understand.

The overall goal on a cruising or a racing boat is to keep all possible sail changing options open and to have the crew ready for any eventuality. Equally important is the ability to anticipate the next sail change.

The immediate goal during a maneuver is to be able to react immediately and without confusion when a sail change is called for, and then to execute that change with minimal disruption. After the maneuver has been completed, the foredeck should be cleared and made ready for the next evolution.

The general principles of halyard organization should be known by everyone on board, if possible. They certainly must be understood by the bowman, who works forward and attaches sheets and halyards to the sail; by the mastman, who works around the mast during the raising and lowering of sails; and by the pitman, who works the winches and also helps in raising and lowering the sails. Each maneuver should be talked through *before* it is executed so that both the plan and the sequence of events are clear. Other crew members can help by making sure that a twist, wrap, or lost halyard is quickly observed and corrected. Communication can be by voice or by hand signal. Here are a few more specific points:

- For an initial jib hoist, always use the center halyard and the leeward groove of the headstay.
- For an initial spinnaker set, hoist the sail on the leeward wing halyard. The weather wing halyard is free for a spinnaker change, and the center halyard is available (after the jib is dropped) for resetting a jib or staysail.
- Lead the halyards forward when you are sailing downwind. After the spinnaker is up and the jib is lowered, keep the center halyard forward at the headstay. Before gybing, bring the third halyard forward; if you don't, it will be trapped behind the spinnaker pole after the gybe.
- During a *peel* change, in which a second spinnaker is set before the first one, keep the starboard halyard to starboard of the port halyard.
- Always color-code halyards to reduce the chances for confusion. Wing halyards also need halyard balls, which lock around the halyard just above the shackle, to prevent them from jamming or scoring halyard sheaves. To color-code, wrap the shackle swage fitting with the appropriate color tape – red to port, green to starboard, for example. For night work, use some form of tactile coding so you feel the difference between halyards in the dark.

In an around-the-buoys race, you would start out using the center halyard and the port (leeward) headstay groove for the jib. This way the port halyard is available for a leeward spinnaker set (assuming the mark rounding is to port), and the starboard halyard is ready for a genoa change on the wind, should it become necessary.

At the windward mark, the pitman should note the jib halyard setting so it can be duplicated when the sail is set again later. Before the spinnaker pole is put in place, the bowman must make sure the starboard halyard, which is still in place at the base of the mast, is clear – that is, to leeward of both the pole and the topping lift. The pitman should check the jib halyard tail to ensure a smooth drop after the spinnaker is up.

Once the spinnaker is up, the jib can come down, and its halyard can be secured at the base of the headstay or pulpit. Furl the lowered jib, but keep it in the pre-feeder, ready to go. If the spinnaker has to be gybed, the bowman should take the starboard halyard forward from the mast base to the headstay before the gybe so it will not be trapped to windward of the pole after the gybe.

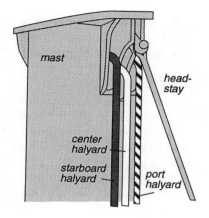

Fig. 1 *A color-coding system for three halyards. The wing-spinnaker halyards use red for port and green for starboard. The center jib halyard is blue. Use the same color tape on the corresponding halyard shackles.*

If a halyard should be trapped on the wrong side of the pole, it can be passed over the top of the pole by shackling it to the jibsheets (which should always be led over the pole) and pulling it over the top of them. However, it's far better to avoid the problem in the first place.

If you approach the leeward mark on port tack, move the spare halyard back to the mast base. After confirming the headsail selection with the tactician, attach the jib head to the center halyard and feed the sail into the port groove. With a leeward takedown, the spinnaker will come down to starboard, and the port halyard will be around the headstay. You can use the port halyard for the next spinnaker set either by setting the chute from the starboard rail or by passing the halyard around the headstay and returning it to the port side of the boat.

When you are sailing upwind with a genoa, conditions can change rapidly. You may need, for example, to change down from the #1. If the tactician agrees to a *tack change* – changing headsails while the boat is coming about – you'll first need to bring the new jib up on deck in its turtle. The bowman attaches the starboard halyard to the head of the sail, moves it forward so the luff can feed into the groove, and attaches the tack. Check carefully aloft to make sure the starboard halyard is not wrapped around the headstay or fouled on the port halyard, which may still be on the starboard side after the spinnaker is doused.

If you are sailing upwind through the fleet, which is still heading for the leeward mark, ideally you should be on starboard tack as you set up for the tack change. After the next jib halyard is in place, the hoist can be started as soon as the weather jibsheet is taken off the old jib and attached to the new jib. Once there's a clear track through the fleet on port tack, start to hoist the new jib; tack as soon as the halyard of the new sail tops out in the full-hoist position.

At that point the bowman moves forward from the mast to the bow pulpit. As soon as the old jib starts to luff as the boat comes into the wind, the halyard for the old jib should be cast off. The sail should be pulled down most of the way before the tack is completed. Once it is neatly piled on deck, put a sail tie around the luff, release the tack from the fitting, and pull the sail aft. Once it reaches the mast, remove the halyard and secure it to the mast collar. The remaining sheet can then be removed, led around the mast, and attached to the new jib. Pass the #1 below, collect the luff, and secure the sail; now it's ready to go again if it's needed.

As you round the windward mark, the usual call is for a bear-away set on starboard tack. In this case, pass the port halyard around the headstay and set it up on the port rail. As you round the mark, hoist the spinnaker and then drop the jib. Once it's down, leave the center and starboard halyards forward and re-lead the jib into the port groove.

If the breeze is fading, you might try gybing onto port and going off on a broad reach. But as the breeze fades even more, the heavy spinnaker you are flying will start to sag. It's time for a peel change.

A *spinnaker peel* is comparable to changing jibs when going upwind. In both cases you hoist the new sail before the old one is dropped. Since the spinnaker is raised on a wing halyard, you always use the other wing halyard. For example, if the spinnaker is on the port halyard and you are on starboard gybe, take the starboard halyard around the headstay, attach it to the new spinnaker, and hoist the new chute *inside* the old one so that the starboard halyard stays to starboard of the port halyard.

If the old spinnaker is on the port halyard and you are on port gybe, you still use the starboard halyard – but now you take it outside and *behind* the old chute. Raise the new chute outside the old chute, and take the old one down inside. Here again, keep the starboard halyard to starboard of the port halyard, leaving the port halyard available for an inside peel. Or you can pass it around the headstay so it is ready for a jib if you need to set one.

In very heavy air, an outside spinnaker set can be a difficult proposition because of the friction between the two sails. In that case, hoist the new chute inside the old one, but use the outside halyard. If you are on port gybe and the spinnaker is on the port halyard, peel with the starboard halyard, using an inside hoist. Then pull the old sail down aft, to starboard and to leeward. This maneuver does trap the port halyard aft, and you'll have to clear the halyard before you use it again. For example, if you take the port halyard directly to the bow, it will be wrapped around the starboard halyard. You have to get the port halyard outside the starboard halyard to clear it.

If you have to peel again, use the trapped port halyard to pull the new chute up on the outside. Then all lines will be cleared once the old spinnaker is down. If you don't do a peel, the trapped halyard can be easily cleared by taking it forward around the headstay once the spinnaker is lowered.

Whenever you peel, and whenever the jib is down, keep the center halyard forward at the headstay clear and ready to use.

Distance racing differs from around-the-buoys competition in that both the race format and the weather are less certain. The best tactical approach is to set the jib on the center halyard and leeward headstay groove and the spinnaker on the leeward wing halyard.

If you have a downwind start under spinnaker, use the leeward wing halyard and keep the center and weather wing halyards forward so they are ready for the next change.

One important detail on a distance race involves watch changes. It is vital that the bowman of one watch give correct information on the status of the halyards to the next watch. Ideally, all the halyards should be in the correct position when the watch changes. However, if anything is amiss – a halyard is behind or under another line, for example – the new watch must be told about it rather than having to find out the hard way. I feel strongly that only the bowman should handle the halyards at the bow; if more than one person is involved on each watch, the chances for confusion are multiplied.

Some boats use only two halyards even though they may have three sheaves aloft, partially to save weight. Two halyards are all you really need unless you want to hoist three headsails at the same time. Some crews rig a light messenger so that a third halyard can be rigged quickly if the need arises. Ideally, all headsail halyards should be interchangeable and capable of being rigged for use with either a spinnaker or a jib.

None of the procedures I've mentioned are complicated as long as you keep the big picture in mind. If you follow the steps I've outlined, you can take advantage of the flexibility a three-halyard and double-grooved headstay system gives you. If you keep the halyards clear, you can set and change headsails as often as you want.

Contributors

John Alofsin is president of J World Sailing schools which are located in Newport, Rhode Island; Key West, Florida; San Diego, California; and Annapolis, Maryland. Twice a collegiate All American, he has won National, North American and World titles in the J/24 and J/22 classes. He lives with his wife Gail in Newport, Rhode Island.

Ed Baird has won world championships in Lasers, J/24s and the International 50-foot Class, and has had top rankings in several other international races. He has also coached Olympic champions and America's Cup contenders. With experience on all types of boats from catamarans to sailboards, he is often asked to speak and write on various sailing subjects. He lives with his wife Lisa and son Max in St. Petersburg, Florida.

Art Bandy is an avid West Coast sailor with a lifetime of expertise in rigging and rigging products. As national sales manager for Forespar Products Corporation, he has been involved in rigging-related product testing and development, trying out new ideas in the numerous regattas and cruises in which he has participated. He is currently involved in the restoration of the classic yacht *Gesture* which was built in 1941.

Steve Benjamin is an Olympic silver medalist in the 470 Class, as well as a three-time world champion in Fireballs and 505s and a former Intercollegiate Sailor of the Year. He helmed in three U.S. entries in the Admiral's Cup, winning the race in the two-ton class in 1991 aboard *Bravura*. He is currently president of Banks Sails USA in Oyster Bay, New York.

Todd Berman is an accomplished racing sailor, including victories as tactician in the 1989 SORC and as part of the winning team at the 1985 J/24 World Championships in Japan. He is currently sales manager at Halsey Sailmakers in Mystic, Connecticut, where he is also sailing instructor for several organizations.

John Collins has been analyzing the intricacies of ocean racing handicapping for more than 20 years. He has been an official PHRF handicapper in New England and elsewhere since 1977, and has sailed in numerous offshore racing events. He also races a Lightning and has won several regional and national level one-design competitions over the years.

Wally Cross runs a sailing business in Grosse Pointe Farms, Michigan, called Total Management, which is a consulting firm that helps match sailmakers and boatbuilders with competitive sailing customers worldwide. He has been a competitive sailor all his life, with his most recent racing efforts focusing on the 1994 Canada's Cup. He was also the manager of North Sails Detroit for many years.

Steve Cruse has competed on winning boats in numerous races including the Bermuda Race, SORC, Block Island Race, Antigua Race, Halifax Race and others. He has also spent extensive time aboard his C&C 41, cruising with his wife and two sons. Since graduating from Boston University, he has worked in the sailmaking business including stints at Doyle and Hood. He is currently the New England sales representative for North Sails, concentrating on cruising sails and innovations.

Steve Dashew and his wife Linda are well-known cruisers, with four books, a video series and numerous performance sailing and cruising articles to their credit. In the 60s and early 70s, Steve concentrated largely on performance sailing, breaking the sailboat speed record in 1971. Then in 1976, with two small daughters aboard, they completed a six-year circumnavigation. They went on to found Deerfoot Yachts, then Sundeer Yachts, both based on their years of cruising and championship racing experience. They currently live in Tucson, Arizona.

Brad Dellenbaugh has a lifetime of coaching and sailing behind him including coaching the sailing team at Brown University from 1980 to 1990 and the U.S. Women's World Team from 1984 to 1987. He has been tapped frequently as tactician and skipper for competitions all over the world, and he writes and illustrates articles for numerous sailing publications. He is currently the offshore sailing coach at the U.S. Naval Academy in Annapolis, Maryland.

Sal Fertitta began sailing Hamptons One-Designs at age 14 and crewed a North American champion in the class by the time he was 16. He then turned to cruising both coastal and offshore, a pursuit he has followed for nearly 45 years. He also participated in the research and development of

DuPont's sailcloth innovations, and is the author of two booklets on sails and one on cordage. He is a frequent contributor to various sailing publications but says he is most happy when cruising and writing about gunkholes and marinas on Chesapeake Bay.

Dave Franzel has taught sailing professionally for more than 20 years. In 1977, he founded the Boston Sailing Center, one of the first organizations to bring sailing to people who don't own boats. His experience includes many years as one of the country's top Sonar and Soling racers, as well as a transatlantic and coastal delivery skipper.

Derrick R. Fries began sailing at age six and went on to win six World Single-Handed Championships in Sunfish and Force 5 class boats, as well as 14 national and North American championships in various single-handed classes. He is the author of four sailing books including *Start Sailing Right.* He is the founder of Windstar Productions, recently received a doctorate in educational administration from the University of Michigan and is currently employed as an assistant principal in the Birmingham, Michigan, public schools.

Bill Gladstone is the author of *Performance Sailing Technique* and a U.S. Sailing judge. He has been teaching sailing and racing for more than 20 years, and is the founder and owner of the Chicago Sailing Club. In the off-season, he provides PHRF, IMS, MORC and One-Design seminars for aspiring competitive sailors. He lives in Evanston, Illinois.

Eric Hall regularly races in IMS competitions, with frequent appearances in the Block Island, Annapolis-Newport, and Bermuda Races. He competes in multihulls as well as monohulls and is the owner of the custom spar-making firm, Hall Spars Inc. of Bristol, Rhode Island.

Robert Hopkins Jr. is a familiar face on the Olympic and America's Cup scene. His most recent efforts include duties as vice president and chief operating officer of the PACT 95 America's Cup campaign. He was also the technology coordinator and navigator for the 1992 Italian America's Cup challenger. He was head coach of the U.S. Olympic Sailing Team in 1984, and planned and directed U.S. Olympic coaching efforts from 1988 to 1992. He lives in Bangor, Maine.

Mike Huck Jr. has sailed in everything from Tall Ships and 65-foot catamarans to E scows and iceboats. He has raced on boats of all types for nearly 25 years, and writes about boating in the off season. His book *Around the Buoys: A Manual of Tactics and Strategy* was published in 1994.

Jeff Johnstone began sailing at the age of five and gained early experience on Lasers, 420s and 470s. But he soon gravitated to J boats, co-founding in 1981 the J World Performance Sailing School in Newport, Rhode Island. He is a top competitor in J/24 Midwinter and World Championships, co-writer and producer of the J World videos on sail trim and tactics, and is president of J Boats Inc. in Newport, Rhode Island.

Tom Leweck is an active racer who has won six National and North American championships in both one-design dinghy and keelboat classes. He is also an ocean racing enthusiast and navigator, with seven Transpac races and more than 50 other major international offshore races in his log. He is a former commodore of the California Yacht Club and is currently a U.S. Sailing senior judge.

Sally Lindsay is a sailmaker and active racer with her most recent efforts in the Doublehanded Pacific Cup in 1990, the Pacific Cup in 1992 and the Doublehanded Ocean Series (first place) in San Francisco in 1993. In between numerous offshore races, she has been designing and making sails since 1969. She has been the owner/president of Precision Technical Sewing in Palo Alto, California, since 1979.

Rob MacLeod is the author of four books on sailing as well as co-host and co-creator of a television series on sailing for public broadcasting television stations in Canada and the United States. He has helped develop the standards used by the Canadian Yachting Association's students and instructors. He has been a professional sailing instructor for 18 years and is based in Hamilton, Ontario.

Peter Mahr is president of North Cloth, a division of North Sails. He is a mechanical engineer by training and joined North in 1979 at the beginning of the revolution in laminated sailcloth development. Products developed under his direction have been used in several America's Cup, Whitbread, SORC and Admiral's Cup races.

Jim Marshall was in his first transatlantic race at the age of 16 and has been in numerous Bermuda, Admiral's Cup, Annapolis-Newport and other ocean races over the years. He is frequently tapped as navigator in these races, and has been a runner up for the Rolex Yachtsman of the Year award. He is currently sales director for Ockum Instruments in Milford, Connecticut, coordinating the design and development of high-performance electronics for various offshore racing efforts. He also writes for several sailing magazines and wrote a textbook for Ockum-sponsored seminars.

Roger Marshall is a yacht designer and racer with numerous offshore competitions under his belt including nine Bermuda and five Fastnet races. He is also the author of five books on sailing and yacht design including his most recent book *Marshall's Marine Source Book*. He worked for the prestigious design firm Sparkman & Stevens before striking out on his own. He was project manager for the *Courageous* challenge in the 1987 America's Cup campaign, and writes regularly for various sailing magazines and newspapers.

Charles Mason has sailed all his life. He is a founding editor of *SAIL* Magazine and is presently its executive editor. He was the editor of *The Best of SAIL Trim*.

Larry Montgomery is a professional marine surveyor who has sailed on both U.S. coasts for 20 years and logged thousands of miles in the process. He has been a marine consultant to naval architects, boatbuilders and sailors, has written scores of articles for boating magazines and is currently president of Montgomery Maritime Survey Inc. in Port Townsend, Washington.

Lin & Larry Pardey are among the best-known cruising couples in the world. Having wandered the world's oceans together since 1969, they are the authors of eight books including the classic *Cruising in Serrafyn*. They have also published four videos and scores of articles focusing on advice on making the most of living aboard a small sailboat. Although they have visited nearly 70 countries from the Orient to the United States, they are still cruising, looking for more countries "and friends" to add to their list.

Scott Rohrer is a native of Seattle with extensive offshore and class boat sailing experience. He has numerous titles in the Six-Meter, Three-Quarter-Ton and Two-Ton classes. He has been an instructor with the North U. sailing seminars for the last 15 years and is currently the head of the Seattle office of Mariners Insurance Group.

Jeff Spranger never let two careers – first as a school teacher then as associate editor of *SAIL* Magazine – interfere with sailing. Starting out in Beetle Cats, Snipes and Rhodes 18s, he eventually moved up to Herreshoff S boats and managed to win a couple of championships. When a growing family put a crimp in one-design racing, he built a 34-foot cruising boat that he continues to race more often than cruise.

Barbara Stetson grew up sailing on Long Island Sound, eventually representing Pequot Junior Yacht Club at the Midget and Girls Championships.

She is currently a teacher of basic sailing, racing, and advanced sailing techniques at the Offshore Sailing School in New York Harbor.

Michael Tamulaites began sailing Sunfish and Lasers as a youngster in the 1970s. He moved up to J/24s and eventually became a sail trimmer aboard the winning 1988 Collegiate Sloop National Championship team. He has been an assistant editor at *SAIL* Magazine since 1990, and is currently the racing editor.

Mike Toppa grew up in the sailing town of Newport, Rhode Island, eventually sailing aboard three America's Cup boats before landing a spot as sail trimmer in the 1992 winning boat from the America³ syndicate. He has been in numerous other offshore races including the Maxi World Championships, Rolex Cup, Sardinia Cup and others. He co-authored *Speed Sailing* with Gary Jobson and is currently the owner of North Sails Florida in Ft. Lauderdale.

Tom Whidden is well known among followers of the America's Cup races and innovations in sailmaking technology. He was tactician aboard *Stars & Stripes* which won the Cup in 1987. He was also skipper aboard four winners of the Bermuda Race, was a U.S. Finn class champion and was five times a class champion in the SORC with an overall win in 1982. He won the Maxi World Championships twice. He took Sobstad Sailmakers from a small one-loft company in Connecticut to the second largest sailmaker in the world. He has also served as president and chief operating officer for North Sails, the world's largest sailmaker. He lives with his wife and two children in Essex, Connecticut.

Tim Yourieff has competed in numerous yacht competitions around the world including one SORC, two Japan Cups, three Sydney-Hobarts, and four Admiral Cup races. He also has extensive experience in one-designs such as the International 505 and Etchells 22. He is currently the manager of the yacht sails division of Neil Pryde Sails.

About the Editor:

Ken Textor has lived and worked aboard boats for nearly two decades. He is the author of *Innocents Afloat*, published by Sheridan House, and a regular contributor to numerous boating magazines. He currently runs a sailing excursion business on Arrowsic Island, Maine.

Index